BAOFENG RADIO MAVERICK

TURN ON WHEN THE WORLD TURNS OFF. A REVOLUTIONARY APPROACH TO BAOFENG RADIO, OFF-GRID COMMUNICATION, AND TECHNOLOGICAL RESILIENCE

MICHAEL R. BROWN

TABLE OF CONTENTS

INTRODUCTION

"5 Be wise in the way you act towards outsiders; make the most of every opportunity. 6 Let your conversations be always full of grace, seasoned with salt, so that you may know how to answer everyone."
Colossians 4:5-6

Founded in 2004, Baofeng is a company that specializes in radio communication. Baofeng has always aimed to create user value through innovation and fulfilling its customer's needs.

Once a small factory of just 30 people, Baofeng company has taken the two-way radio market by storm, creating affordable technology and accessories at a fraction of the cost of its competitor. Today, the company leads with one, powerful tenet in mind: "Customer first, service first, reputation first." Their products are sold all over the world and follow the highest manufacturing standards. Some of them also passed the CE certification of the European Telecommunications Standards Committee and the RoHS certification in 2011, which gives them a solid foundation in the European market.

To retrace Baofeng's journey, we need to go back to the moment of its creation. It was in 2001, in the Chinese province of Fujian when a team of visionary engineers led by CEO Zheng Guangming were toiling to develop the field of two-way radio technology. Little did they know that their innovations would revolutionize the industry, becoming a byword for affordability, reliability, and expertise.

Fujian Nan'an Baofeng Electronics Co. Ltd, Baofeng's parent company, was founded in 1993 and specialized in the manufacture of wireless communications equipment. However, it wasn't until 2000 that the company became a separate entity.

In 2001, Baofeng unveiled its very first product—the UV-3R handheld transceiver. A pioneer in dual-band technology, this handheld was sold to the general public at an affordable price and was revered by early consumers. It paved the way for the brand's meteoric rise to become a key player in the two-way radio market.

This genuine success led Baofeng down the path of innovation, buoyed by the determination to constantly push the boundaries of radio communication. With each new product, the company aims to democratize access to cutting-edge technology, while meeting the different needs of potential buyers (amateur radio operators, emergency radio operators, young users, and so on).

In 2012, Baofeng experienced a real turning point with the release of its UV-5R series, a line of handheld transceivers. Its ergonomic design and innovative functions definitively sealed the company's innovative position in the radio communication market.

Baofeng offers a variety of radios to meet consumer needs. Here is a non-exhaustive list of some of the models for sale.

- **BTECH UV-82C:** Suitable for Private Land Mobile Radio Services (PLMRS). They are made for professional purposes by public safety agencies, utilities, railroads, manufacturers, and other businesses. A license is required to use it.

- **BTECH GMRS-V2:** Suitable for General Mobile Radio Services (GMRS). These handheld radios are only made for personnel use. They only cover a short distance and allow short data messaging and GPS location information. A license is required to use them and covers the immediate family of the licensee.

- **BTECH MURS-V2:** Suitable for Multi-Use Radio Services (MURS). These types of radios are not connected to the public telephone network or used with repeaters. Thus, they only display a very short range of applications. They are generally locked to MURS channels and really easy to use, which makes them a good option even for children. No license is required to use them.

- **BTECH FRS-A1:** Suitable for Family Radio Services (FRS). Very similar to GMRS, they have the advantage of not requiring a license. They also can be used for professional and personal purposes. They are limited to narrowband modulation and are generally locked to FRS channels which makes them child-friendly. Moreover, these UHF radios provide better coverage to communicate inside buildings or in the woods.

- **BTECH UV-5X3:** Suitable for Amateur Radio Services (ARS). These radios can operate a variety of frequencies including HF, VHF, and UHF. To use them, you have to pass a license test. They cannot be used for commercial purposes. It is the most versatile option when it comes to frequency availability and selection.

We will now compare the strengths and weaknesses of Baofeng with other brands in the market of radio communication.

Baofeng	
Strengths	**Weaknesses**
Affordable price *Renowned for its very economical radios, making them accessible to a wide audience.*	**Manufacturing quality** *Lower prices often mean less robust products.*
Rich features *Models like the Baofeng UV-5R offer an impressive range of features, including a wide frequency range, good memory capacity, and customization options.*	**Legal compliance** *Baofeng radios do not always comply with local regulations concerning the power of authorized frequencies. Therefore, the user must be very vigilant to avoid any legal problems.*
A wide range of products offering great versatility of use *Baofeng offers an impressive range of products tailored to the specific needs of potential buyers. So there is something for everyone.*	

Yaesu	
Strengths	**Weaknesses**
High-quality products *Renowned for its long-lasting, robust equipment.*	**High price** *Price much higher than other models on the market.*
Rich features and great performance *Excellent audio quality, wide range, and reliability. These products offer many advanced features.*	**The complexity of use** *Equipment can be difficult to use for beginners.*

Kenwood	
Strengths	**Weaknesses**
High-quality products *Renowned for its long-lasting, robust equipment.*	**High price** *Price much higher than other models on the market.*
Audio quality *Excellent audio clarity and performance, even in difficult operating conditions.*	**Less versatility of use** *These products offer fewer adjustable features than other models on the market.*
Customer service *Renowned for its excellent customer service and technical support.*	

Motorola	
Strengths	**Weaknesses**
Reputation and reliability World leader in the communications industry.	**High price** (These products are among the most expensive on the market.
Cutting-edge technologies These features enable clear and secure communications.	**Weight and size** Some professional models can be heavy and bulky.)
Customer service Excellent technical support and availability of replacement parts.	

As you can see, Baofeng is an excellent option for users looking for a cost-effective, feature-rich solution. However, you need to be aware of the compromises in terms of regulatory compliance.

Now let's go through some real-life examples in which your best two-way radio can be of great use. Each customer group has specific needs in terms of range, robustness, security, and additional features, which influence their choice of brand and model for this kind of equipment.

In the professional environment:

Safety and rescue professionals: Used for fast, reliable communications in emergencies, these users often choose products with advanced features such as water and shock resistance, and secure channels. They need radios to communicate instantaneously to coordinate themselves on the ground and quickly manage any incidents that may occur.

Industry and construction: Rugged and robust radios are required for team coordination, often on large sites where fast, clear communication is crucial but could include structures that affect transmission quality.

Agriculture: Farm workers use radios to coordinate work on large farms, often in areas where telephone coverage is limited. They require reliable, long-range communication options.

Military and law enforcement: Soldiers and police officers use radios for tactical communications on the ground, requiring robust, secure equipment. They need encrypted radios with advanced features to set up discreet and secure operations.

Transport and logistics: Truck drivers use radios for transport coordination, route management, and communication with operational bases. At airports and ports, staff use radios to coordinate ground operations, ensure security, and manage the flow of passengers and goods.

Retail: Employees in these companies may use radios for communication between security personnel, maintenance teams, and managers.

Personal activities:

Hobbies: Radios can be used by groups engaged in activities such as hiking, mountaineering, camping, and motorized sports for communication in remote areas. Likewise, hunters or fishermen use them to communicate for safety and coordination of activities.

Travel and expeditions: These devices are essential for communication in remote or mountainous areas, where cell phones don't work.

Personal safety: Radios are useful for communications in the event of natural disasters or other emergencies during which telephone networks are disrupted.

Amateur radio: Radio enthusiasts often use two-way radios to communicate with other enthusiasts, take part in radio events, and conduct experiments with these technologies.

Outdoor games and family time: Kids can use walkie-talkies for role-playing, treasure hunts, and outdoor adventures. Radios are handy for parents to keep in touch with children when they're playing outdoors or in a park.

Navigation: Seamen use these devices for communication between crew members or between different boats when out on the sea, lakes, or rivers. They can also be useful in the event of damage or shipwreck, to alert rescue services in the absence of a phone network.

Communication plays an essential part in our lives. No matter what circumstances or situations we find ourselves in, we need to be able to communicate with others. The Internet or the telephone network, for example, enables us to talk to someone on the other side of the planet. But what do you do when you're deprived of these means of communication?

Baofeng radios offer you an alternative to grid-dependent technologies, allowing you to communicate in the most extreme of environments—if you know how—so let's get into it.

Your Gift

Baofeng is a remarkably robust addition to any communication maverick's arsenal. What has endured many to these models is the adaptability of this little handheld. Users do not need to spend a fortune on finicky add-ons and gadgets to maximize the potential and protection of their Baofeng, and with a little ingenuity, you can create your own hybrid radio.

It's precisely this ingenuity that has inspired your gift, DIY Radio Accessories Guide. By scanning the QR code below, you gain access to your complete guide to creating homemade accessories to enhance the functionality of Baofeng radios, including antennas, mounts, and carrying cases.

CHAPTER 1: UNDERSTANDING YOUR BAOFENG RADIO

As you now know, Baofeng has revolutionized the transceiver radio marketplace. Whether you are a professional looking for a reliable means of communication, a lover of outdoor adventures, or an enthusiast of radio communication modes, Baofeng's wide range of two-way radio products offers a solution for every need.

These radios are built with high-end components providing meticulously thought-out functions and optimized performance. From the robust outer casing to the complex internal circuitry, every element plays a crucial role in ensuring clear and reliable communication. To exploit the full potential of these devices, you will need to understand the role Baofeng plays in the marketplace as well as each of its core components.

Baofeng radios are renowned for their great versatility as they offer a wide range of features for different frequency bands, including VHF (Very High Frequency) and UHF (Ultra High Frequency).

Furthermore, these radios display advanced features that go beyond basic communication. These features include memory channels, scan modes, and customizable settings, enabling you to tailor your device to your specific needs, and ensuring a personalized communication experience.

This chapter introduces you to all the information you need to operate your Baofeng radio. So grab your Baofeng radio and get ready to experiment as you learn to communicate with the dynamic world of radio airwaves that surrounds you!

THE COMPONENTS AND ANATOMY OF A BAOFENG RADIO

To understand how your unit works and effectively operate it, you must get accustomed to its physical components and their respective functions. This overall knowledge will also help you troubleshoot any potential issues that arise and provide you with a good grounding for maintaining your radio.

Let's begin by exploring each of the components of atypical Baofeng radio:

1. **Antenna**: This key element enables the transmission and reception of radio signals. Baofeng devices often feature removable antennas to make their replacement easier. For an optimal signal strength and communication range, you

have to choose it wisely and think carefully about its positioning.

2. **Display Screen**: Most Baofeng radios feature a digital screen providing important information such as frequency, channel, battery level, and so on. It serves as the main interface to control the device and customize its parameters.

3. **Keypad**: This is the main input method for controlling your radio. It generally consists of several buttons and knobs that allow you to navigate menus, change channels, adjust volume, and access advanced functions.

4. **Speaker**: The speaker is the audio output component of your radio and enables you to hear incoming transmissions and other audio signals. Baofeng radios are often equipped with high-quality speakers designed to deliver crisp and clear sound, even in noisy environments.

5. **Microphone**: This element captures your voice during transmissions. Baofeng radios generally feature built-in microphones, but some models can also be connected to external microphones for improved audio quality or hands-free operation.

6. **Battery Compartment**: Baofeng radios are powered by rechargeable batteries, which are placed in a dedicated compartment. Ensuring that your batteries are properly maintained and charged is essential to keep your radio running smoothly and increase its operational lifespan.

Basic Functions

*Now that we have covered the various components that make up your radio, let's move on to the basic functions that will enable you t*o communicate effectively.

Powering up and adjusting volume:

1. Before you begin, you will need to ensure your battery is fully charged and ready for us. Make sure to follow manufacturer guidelines for your first charge.

2. Once your battery is charged, locate the power button. For Baofeng, this is usually the volume control button that can be turned clockwise to power on.

3. If this is your first time switching your Baofeng on, it may take a few seconds for the display screen to light up. A message should indicate that the radio is powering on.

4. Once the device is on, use the volume knob or buttons to adjust the sound volume to a comfortable level.

5. Make sure it is loud enough to hear incoming transmissions clearly without drowning out the surrounding noises.

Setting Frequencies:

Baofeng radios operate on different frequencies, each with specific characteristics and conditions of use. The correct frequency setting is essential to establish communication with other devices on the same band.

Manual Frequency Selection: Use the keypad or buttons to navigate to the frequency menu on your radio's display. Manually enter the desired frequency, making sure the band is appropriate for the intended use (e.g. VHF for short-range communications or UHF for longer-range communications).

Memory Channels: Many Baofeng radios feature a function for storing frequently used frequencies in memory channels for quick access. Consult your radio manual to find out how to program and recall these channels.

It is essential to get used to operating with the different frequency bands and their specific uses. For example, the VHF band (136-174 MHz) is commonly used for short-range communications, while the UHF band (400-520 MHz) offers greater range but may require more power. For your exclusive step-by-step guide on how to program and set frequencies, consult Chapter 2.

Accessing Functions and Menu Options:

Baofeng radios are equipped with a keypad to access various features and menu options. While some specific buttons may vary from one model to another, here are some common functions of all the brand's devices:

1. **Scan Mode**: To automatically search for active frequencies within a predefined range.

2. **Programming**: To configure memory channels and tailor settings.

3. **Keypad Lock**: To prevent accidental button presses.

4. **Squelch Adjustment**: To filter out background noises and unwanted interferences.

5. **Power Level**: To preserve battery life or increase the range of transmission.

As each of the chapters unfold, I'll introduce you to each of the functions as well as provide you with instructions. For now, I encourage you to begin getting used to operating your device so that the most basic functions become more intuitive.

THE KEY FEATURES OF BAOFENG RADIOS

Baofeng captured the marketplace by manufacturing reliable, robust, affordable, and easy-to-use two-way radio equipment. This doesn't mean that their radios aren't packed with an array of advanced features that allow their radios to stand out from their competitors.

Dual-Band Capability

One of the main functions of many Baofeng radios is their dual-band capability that enables them to operate simultaneously on VHF and UHF frequencies. This versatility is quality for both professional and amateur uses, as it provides access to continuous communication on different frequencies without the need for separate devices.

For example, a rescue team may use the VHF band for local communications while simultaneously monitoring the UHF band for updates from a central command center. This dual functionality ensures efficient coordination and quick response.

Emergency Alert Functions

In dangerous situations, every second counts. Baofeng radios feature emergency alert functions to guarantee your safety. At the touch of a button, you can instantly send distress signals or activate emergency channels to alert your contacts or the emergency services in your vicinity.

This function is particularly valued by outdoor enthusiasts venturing into remote areas, as well as by professionals working in dangerous environments, as it provides a reliable and efficient way to call for help when needed.

Built-in Flashlight and VOX Mode

Baofeng radios are designed with convenience and practicality in mind. Many models feature an integrated flashlight, allowing the user to light the surrounding area when the night falls. This practical feature can be a lifesaver in emergencies or when moving around in dark environments.

In addition, VOX (Voice-Operated Exchange) mode enables hands-free operation. Thanks to the VOX feature, you can communicate while keeping your hands free for other tasks. This feature is particularly useful for professionals who need to multitask. It can also be useful in the event of danger when users need to use their hands to ensure their safety.

Squelch Control and Signal Filtering

To maintain clear communication, you will have to filter out unwanted background noises and interferences. Baofeng radios feature a squelch control that enables you to adjust the sensitivity of the receiver and reduce stray sounds.

When correctly set, the squelch attenuates unwanted noise while the radio is not receiving a useful signal. If its level is too low, you will hear a static noise. Whereas if it is too high, you may not hear the faintest transmissions. Adjusting the squelch is all about finding the perfect balance for clear communications without excessive background noise.

This function is particularly useful when radios are used in noisy environments, such as construction sites or crowded events, where background noise is likely to interfere with communications.

With the features of your Baofeng now slightly better understood, it's time to move on to getting started with your handheld, and learning the basics that will have you transmitting over the airwaves in no time.

CHAPTER 2: GETTING STARTED—FIRST STEPS WITH YOUR BAOFENG

Once your Baofeng is powered up, some additional steps need to be taken to ensure your radio is functioning correctly. These include assembling parts, like your antenna, belt clip, battery, and any other accessories you've purchased, and beginning the process of programming your channels.

In addition, you need to know what to do if something goes wrong, not just when you power your device up, but as you begin using it daily. Like any other piece of equipment, Baofeng can encounter some pretty common issues. Rest assured, these obstacles are easy to troubleshoot your way through.

UNBOXING AND INITIAL SETUP

Unboxing your brand new Baofeng radio is a moment filled with excitement. However, it is important to do this methodically to ensure that every element is in perfect condition.

Carefully remove any additional items from your box and check that they have not been damaged during shipping.

These items should include your radio unit which you've powered on, a rechargeable battery that has been charged for 12 hours, a belt clip, a wrist strap, a user manual, and various other accessories depending on the model.

Let's proceed with assembling your radio.

1. **Installing the battery:** If you haven't yet installed your battery to power on your radio, now is the time to charge the battery. Once charged, locate the battery compartment at the back of your device. Open the cover and insert the rechargeable battery, making sure it is facing the right way and that you're sliding the battery in carefully. Don't force the battery into its compartment.

2. **Attaching the antenna:** Most Baofeng radios are equipped with a removable antenna. Carefully screw the antenna onto the connector on the top of the radio. Make sure it is firmly attached to optimize signal reception and transmission.

3. **Belt clip and wrist strap**: If you have these accessories, you can attach them to your radio unit to make it easier to carry and avoid accidental falls. Make sure to follow the manufacturer's guidelines to prevent damaging or overheating your radio.

Note: Before or after assembling your radio, it is essential to charge the battery fully before your first use. Refer to your user manual for specific instructions on charging, as the process may differ based on the model and battery specification.

Below are some basic guidelines for charging your battery.

Use the approved charger or charging cable supplied with your Baofeng radio.

Plug it into a power source and place the battery or radio into the charging dock.

Check the indicators (LEDs or display prompts) to make sure it is correctly charging.

Wait for the battery to be fully charged before removing it.

Taking good care of your battery and recharging it properly is essential for preserving optimum functioning and ensuring the lifespan of your Baofeng radio.

PROGRAMMING FREQUENCIES

Effective radio communication mainly depends on the proper programming of your required frequencies. This can be done manually on your device or using dedicated programming software. Let's look at these two options in detail.

Manual Frequency Programming

Manual programming implies entering frequencies directly onto your radio using the keypad or control buttons.

Let's begin with how to manually program a simplex channel. Access the frequency programming menu on your radio's display by navigating the menu options or using the predefined shortcuts.

1. **Press [VFO/MR] and enter *Frequency Mode.***

2. **Press [A/B] and choose the *A-Side* (upper display).**
   The A side must be used to program channels into your unit. Any data entered on the B Side will not be saved.

3. **Press [BAND] for the frequency band.**
   Toggle [BAND] to choose 136 MHz (VHF) or 470 MHz (UHF).
   If you choose a band that does not match the frequency you will enter in step 5, the radio will cancel the operation.

4. **Disable TDR (*Dual Watch/Dual Standby*).**
   Press [MENU] 7 [MENU] [press up/down arrow keys] OFF [MENU] [EXIT]

It is highly advisable to turn TDR off when programming directly from the radio.

5. **Enter the frequency**
   Use the keypad to enter the desired frequency into the radio. Make sure you use the correct format and that you are operating within the authorized frequency ranges.

6. ***Optional:*** You may also need to set specific parameters such as offset frequencies (for repeater operation) or CTCSS/DCS tones (for selective calling). **Enter the transmit CTCSS/DCS code.**

   ◇ CTCSS - [MENU] 13 [MENU] [enter/choose code XXXX] [MENU] [EXIT]
   ◇ DCS - [MENU] 12 [MENU] [choose code XXXXX] [MENU] [EXIT]

7. **Assign the frequency to a channel.**
   [MENU] 27 [MENU] [enter channel number XXX] [MENU] [EXIT]

Let's continue with how to manually program a repeater channel.

1. **Press [VFO/MR] and enter *Frequency Mode*.**

2. **Press [A/B] and choose the** A Side **(upper display).**
   As for the simplex channels, the A side must be used to program the repeater channels into your unit. Any data entered on the B Side will not be saved.

3. **Press [BAND] for the frequency band**
   Toggle [BAND] to choose 136 MHz (VHF) or 470 MHz (UHF).
   If you choose a band that does not match the frequency you will enter in step 7, the radio will cancel the operation.

4. Optional: **Clear any CTCSS/DCS codes previously assigned to the channel.**
   If no previous codes exist or if you are setting up the channel for the first time and no codes are needed, set the menu items listed below to **OFF**.

   ◇ RX DCS - [MENU] 10 [MENU] [enter 0 (OFF)] [MENU] [EXIT]
   ◇ RX CTCSS - [MENU] 11 [MENU] [enter 0 (OFF)] [MENU] [EXIT]
   ◇ TX DCS - [MENU] 12 [MENU] [enter 0 (OFF)] [MENU] [EXIT]
   ◇ TX CTCSS - [MENU] 13 [MENU] [enter 0 (OFF)] [MENU] [EXIT]

5. **Disable TDR (**DualWatch/Dual Standby**).**
   Press [MENU] 7 [MENU] [press up/down arrow keys] OFF [MENU] [EXIT]
   It is highly advised to turn TDR off when programming directly from the radio.

6. Optional: **Delete any existing data on the channel to program.**
   Skip this step if you are setting up the channel for the first time.

Press [MENU] 28 [press up/down arrow keys to choose channel number] [MENU] [EXIT]

7. **Enter the repeater output (your receiving) frequency.**
Use the keypad to enter the frequency into the radio.

8. **Input the repeater frequency offset.**
Press [MENU] 26 [MENU] [enter the offset for 2 meters or 70 cm repeater] [MENU] [EXIT]

9. **Enter the Transmit Frequency Shift.**
Press [MENU] 25 [MENU] [enter 1 for positive shift or 2 for negative shift] [MENU] [EXIT]

10. Optional: **Enter the transmit CTCSS/DCS code.**

   ❖ CTCSS – [MENU] 13 [MENU] [enter/choose code XXXX] [MENU] [EXIT]
   ❖ DCS – [MENU] 12 [MENU] [choose code XXXXX] [MENU] [EXIT]

11. **Assign the receive frequency entered in Step 7 to the channel.**
[MENU] 27 [MENU] [enter channel number XXX] [MENU] [EXIT]

12. **Press the [*Scan] button to activate** Reverse Mode **and display the transmit frequency.**

13. **Assign the transmit frequency to the channel.**
Press [MENU] 27 [MENU] [enter the same memory channel entered in step 12] [MENU] [EXIT]

14. **Press the [*Scan] button to exit** Reverse Mode**.**

To add more channels, you just have to repeat these steps. If you follow them correctly, you should be able to program all 128 channels available on your Baofeng radio.

Although manual programming is straightforward, it can be time-consuming, especially when you need to program multiple frequencies or make frequent changes. This is where programming software can come in very handy.

Programming Software Options

Several software programs are available for Baofeng radios, enabling you to manage and program frequencies more efficiently. One of the most popular options is CHIRP (Computer Aided Radio Programming), an open-source software compatible with a wide range of radio models.

Using programming software like CHIRP offers several advantages:

1.   **Frequency list management:** You can create, edit, and organize your frequency lists directly on your computer, making it easy to manage large sets of channels.

2.   **Cloning and backup:** Thanks to this kind of software, you can create backup files of your radio's settings, making it easy to restore or clone them on other devices.

3.   **Automated programming:** Instead of manually entering frequencies, you can download pre-configured frequency lists from online repositories or create your own, and transfer them to your radio with just a few clicks.

Here's how to get started with your programming software:

1. Download and install the software on your computer.

2. https://baofengtech.com/software/

3. Connect your Baofeng radio via a USB cable or a compatible programming cable. You may need to buy a cable as some models come with it but others do not. You can find it either on Amazon or at your local authorized Baofeng dealer.

4. Launch CHIRP, click on the Radio menu, and choose Download From Radio. The Clone window will open.

5. Select the serial port you want to use from the Drop down menu.

6. Select the correct Vendor and (if required) the appropriate Model.

7. Click OK to start the download process. Clone-mode radios will display a progress bar indicating how much of the image has been downloaded. Live-mode radios will immediately jump to the memory editor and begin to populate it with memories as they are downloaded from the radio.

8. You now have access to your radio's current configuration. You can create an initial backup file.

9. You can proceed to edit your frequency list and make any additions, deletions, or modifications you wish. This step can be done manually or by importing data from other sources.

10. If you are using a clone-mode radio, you may wish to save all these changes in a .img file before moving on to the next step.

11. If you are using a live-mode device, the modifications will automatically be saved on your radio. In this case, the programming process stops here.

12. Once you are done working on this list, you have to upload the file back to the radio. With your image open, go to the Radio menu and choose Upload To Radio. The Vendor and Model are already known, so all you need to do is choose a serial port.

Many programming software options offer user-friendly interfaces, making it easy to navigate and customize settings. Some of them even provide additional features like creating customized codeplugs or importing data from other sources.

Using programming software enables you to simplify the frequency programming process, ensuring accurate and efficient configuration of your Baofeng radio for optimal communication.

BASIC TROUBLESHOOTING

Even the most reliable Baofeng radios can sometimes experience problems, especially when operated by beginners. Getting acquainted with fundamental troubleshooting methods can assist you in promptly recognizing and addressing typical issues.

Common Issues and Solutions

Difficulty Receiving Signals:

- Make sure that the radio is set on the correct frequency and mode (e.g., FM, NFM).
- Check the antenna connection and make sure it is securely attached.
- Adjust the squelch level to an appropriate setting to filter out background noise.
- Move to a different location with better signal coverage or less interference.

Programming Errors:

Poor Audio Quality:

- Adjust the volume level.
- Check for any obstructions or debris covering the speaker or microphone.
- Make sure that the microphone is not too close or too far from your mouth.
- Replace the speaker or microphone if they are damaged or malfunctioning.

Keypad or Button Malfunctions:

- Remove the battery and disconnect any external power sources before reconnecting them to reset the radio.
- Clean the keypad and buttons with a soft cloth or compressed air to remove any dirt or debris.
- If the issue persists, the keypad or buttons may have to be repaired or replaced.

Resetting to Factory Settings

If you face ongoing problems that cannot be fixed with simple troubleshooting steps, resetting your Baofeng radio back to its original factory settings might be required. This will bring back the original settings and might fix software issues or erase any corrupted data.

Refer to your user manual for detailed instructions on how to execute a factory reset on your Baofeng radio model. But here is the usual process to do it.

- **VFO Reset**
1. Turn on the radio and press the MENU button.

2. Press the UP and DOWN arrow key to select RESET.

3. Press MENU to choose RESET.

4. Press the DOWN arrow key to choose VFO.

5. Press MENU. The radio will display [SOURCE?].

6. Press MENU to confirm. The radio will display [WAIT...] for a few seconds, then beep twice to confirm reset is complete. The radio will be back to Chinese language mode.

- **FULL Reset**
1. Turn on the radio and press the MENU button.

2. Press the UP and DOWN arrow key to select RESET.

3. Press MENU to choose RESET.

4. Press the DOWN arrow key to choose ALL.

5. Press MENU. The radio will display [SOURCE?].

6. Press MENU to confirm. The radio will display [WAIT...] for a few seconds, then beep twice to confirm reset is complete. The radio will be back to Chinese language mode.

- **To set language from Chinese to English**
1. Press MENU.

2. Press the UP and DOWN arrow key to select VOICE (Menu Item 14).

3. Press MENU to choose VOICE.

4. Press the DOWN arrow key to choose ENG.

5. Press MENU to choose ENG.

Keep in mind that conducting a factory reset will delete all personalized settings, channels, and other stored data on your radio. Therefore, we recommend using programming software to create a backup file of your radio's configuration before proceeding.

Before you move on to the more advanced features available to you, I'd like to reiterate the importance of your initial configuration of your radio. Taking the time to go through every setup step lays a solid foundation for optimal performance and preserves the longevity of your device. Once you've got the basics under your belt, it's time to move on to learning the language needed to communicate on the airwaves and more advanced features.

CHAPTER 3: ADVANCED OPERATIONS AND FEATURES

Now that you have successfully set up your Baofeng radio and grasped the fundamentals of operation, it is time to dive deeper into the advanced features this powerful device has to offer. Unlocking the full potential of your radio requires exploring and mastering these capabilities.

Baofeng radios are packed with a range of sophisticated functions designed to enhance your communication experience and broaden the scope of what you can achieve. From advanced scanning techniques to customize your monitoring preferences, to innovative signaling systems that facilitate seamless communication across groups, these radios boast an impressive array of tools.

You will gain greater control, flexibility, and performance from your device, allowing you to tackle even the most demanding communication scenarios with confidence.

Throughout this chapter, you will be introduced to these powerful capabilities, providing step-by-step instructions and insights to help you harness and elevate your Baofeng radio use.

Using the Repeater Function

One of the most powerful features of Baofeng radios is the ability to access and utilize repeater systems. Repeaters are specialized radio systems that receive signals on one frequency and retransmit them on another, effectively extending the communication range beyond what a single radio can achieve.

The repeater function serves a crucial purpose for radio users who need to communicate over long distances or in areas with obstructions that would otherwise block or weaken their signals.

Setting Up Repeater Access

To access a repeater system with your Baofeng radio, you will need to program the appropriate frequencies and settings. Here is a step-by-step guide:

1. Identify the repeater input and output frequencies for your area. These can often be found online or through local radio clubs.

2. Program the repeater output frequency (the one you'll be receiving on) into your radio's memory channel.

3. Set the correct offset frequency, which is the difference between the input and output frequencies. Common offsets are 0.6 MHz for 2m (VHF) and 5 MHz for 70cm (UHF) bands.

4. Configure the shift direction (positive or negative) based on whether the input frequency is higher or lower than the output.

5. If required, set the appropriate CTCSS or DCS tones to access the repeater system.

For detailed instructions on programming repeaters to your Baofeng, refer to the "Programming Frequencies" section in Chapter 2.

Finding Repeater Frequencies

Locating active repeater frequencies in your area is essential for effectively using this feature. Here is how:

- Check online repeater databases and directories, which often list frequencies by location. Here is a list of some major websites where you can find them:
  - ❖ Repeaterbook
    https://www.repeaterbook.com/
    Features: Comprehensive database with worldwide coverage, user-submitted data, mobile app available.
  - ❖ RadioReference
    https://www.radioreference.com/
    Features: Extensive database including repeaters, frequencies, and trunked radio systems, forums for community interaction.
  - ❖ RFinder
    https://androiddmr.com/
    Features: Worldwide repeater directory, subscription-based service, integrated with various radio software and devices.
  - ❖ D-Star Info
    http://www.dstarinfo.com/

Features: Focused on D-Star repeaters, including registration tools, maps, and updates.

❖ Ham Radio 360 Repeater Directory
https://hamradio360.com/
Features: User-friendly interface, search by location, frequency, and mode.

❖ The Wireless Institute of Australia
https://www.wia.org.au/members/repeaters/data/
Features: Comprehensive listing of repeaters in Australia, searchable by state and frequency.

❖ UK Repeater
https://ukrepeater.net/
Features: Database specifically for repeaters in the United Kingdom, includes status and operational details.

- ◆ New Zealand Association of Radio Transmitters (NZART)
  https://www.nzart.org.nz/info/repeater-maps
  Features: This site provides an extensive and up-to-date list of repeaters in New Zealand, including maps, frequency pairs, and other relevant details.

- Join local radio clubs or forums, as members can provide valuable information about nearby repeaters.

- Listen for repeater identifiers when scanning frequencies to detect active systems. These signals or information help you identify and differentiate individual repeaters in the amateur radio network. Here are their key components:
  - ◆ **Call Sign**: This is assigned by the relevant regulatory authority and identifies the licensee or owner of the repeater. For example, a repeater might have a call sign like "W1XYZ."
  - ◆ **Frequency Pair**: Composed of an input frequency (on which the repeater receives signals) and an output frequency (on which it transmits), this identifier determines how users access the repeater.
  - ◆ **Offset**: This is the difference between the input and output frequencies. They are generally set at +600 kHz or -600 kHz for VHF and ±5 MHz for UHF.
  - ◆ **CTCSS/DCS Tones**: Continuous Tone-Coded Squelch System (CTCSS) and Digital-Coded Squelch (DCS) tones are sub-audible tones used to access the repeater. They prevent interference from other devices and ensure that only users with the correct tone can use the repeater.
  - ◆ **Location**: The geographic location, often specified by city, region, or specific coordinates, helps users understand its coverage area.
  - ◆ **Mode of Operation**: The mode or technology used by the repeater (FM, D-STAR, DMR, System Fusion, etc…) indicates the type of signals it can handle and ensures compatibility with the user's equipment.

- Some radios or software may include pre-loaded repeater frequency lists for major areas.

Setting Up Repeater Access

To harness the power of repeaters, you'll need to program the specific repeater frequencies into your Baofeng device. Most repeaters operate on two separate frequencies—one for transmitting and another for receiving signals. There is also a predetermined offset between these two frequencies.

Here is how to configure your radio for repeater operation:

1. Access the Repeater Settings menu on your radio's display.

2. Set the Repeater Mode to ON and choose the offset direction (positive or negative).

3. Enter the specific repeater output frequency you want to communicate on.

4. The radio will automatically set the input frequency based on the offset you selected.

Be sure to choose transmission power settings appropriate for communicating via repeaters to ensure optimal performance.

Repeater Etiquette

When using repeater systems, it is important to follow proper etiquette to ensure smooth and respectful communication. Here are some of the steps to follow when it comes to repeater etiquette.

- Listen before transmitting to avoid interrupting ongoing conversations.
- Keep transmissions brief and to the point, allowing others to join the conversation. Do not forget to mark a pause between exchanges.
- Identify yourself and the repeater you are using at the beginning and end of each transmission.
- Avoid discussing prohibited or illegal topics over the repeater system.
- Be courteous and respectful to other users at all times.
- Avoid tying up repeaters unnecessarily
- Never transmit coded signals, music, or unauthorized data

Following these guidelines and leveraging the power of repeater functions effectively allows you to unlock a whole new level of communication capabilities with your Baofeng radio.

Setting Up and Using CTCSS/DCS Codes

In crowded radio environments or areas with multiple users, interference, and cros-stalk can become a significant issue, making it challenging to maintain clear and se-cure communication. Fortunately, Baofeng radios offer advanced features like CTCSS (Continuous Tone-Coded Squelch System) and DCS (Digital-Coded Squelch) codes to mitigate these problems and facilitate more selective calling.

CTCSS and DCS codes are sub-audible tones or digital codes that are transmitted along with your voice signal. These codes act as a form of "electronic key," allowing your radio to only open its squelch and receive transmissions with the matching tone or code. This effectively reduces interference from other signals and unwanted radio traffic, ensuring you only hear communications intended for your particular group or channel.

Programming CTCSS/DCS Codes

CTCSS stands for Continuous, Tone-Coded Squelch System. It is used to allow repe-aters and radio devices to receive particular signals and reject others. The signals that they will receive include a specific sub-audible tone, called a CTCSS tone, that has been added to the signal. Note that you have to program your device to respond to the tone of the respective repeater to access the latter. Without this setup, you will not be able to access the repeater even though your radio may be transmitting and receiving on the correct frequencies. This feature helps reduce interference and enables selective calling. Using these tones also prevents interference from other re-peaters that use the same repeater frequency pair.

Here is how to program the appropriate codes:

1. Access the CTCSS or DCS menu on your radio (refer to your user manual for specific menu navigation).

2. Select the desired CTCSS tone frequency (typically ranging from 67.0 Hz to 254.1 Hz) or DCS code (a three or four-digit number).

3. Set the selected tone or code for both transmit (TX) and receive (RX) functions to ensure compatibility with other radios or repeaters using the same system.

It is important to note that CTCSS tones and DCS codes cannot be used interchan-geably. All radios in your communication group must be set to either CTCSS or DCS, using the same tone frequency or code for seamless communication.

Choosing the Right Codes

Selecting appropriate CTCSS/DCS codes is crucial for effective communication and avoiding interference. Here are some tips:

1. Check with local radio clubs or online resources to determine commonly used codes in your area, as using a unique code can help minimize unintentional interference.

2. Ensure that the codes you select are compatible with any repeaters or radios you plan to communicate with.

3. Avoid using common or well-known codes, as they may be heavily shared and prone to interference.

4. If you experience persistent interference, consider changing to a different CTCSS tone or DCS code.

There are 55 standard CTCSS tones:

67	97.4	141.3	177.3	213.8
69.3	100	146.2	179.9	218.1
71.9	103.5	150	183.5	221.3
74.4	107.2	151.4	186.2	225.7
77	110.9	156.7	189.9	229.1
79.7	114.8	159.8	192.8	233.6
82.5	118.8	162.2	196.6	237.1
85.4	123	165.5	199.5	241.8
88.5	127.3	167.9	203.5	245.5
91.5	131.8	171.3	206.5	250.3
94.8	136.5	173.8	210.7	254.1

By properly setting up and utilizing CTCSS/DCS codes, you can significantly improve the clarity and security of your radio communications, ensuring that your transmissions are received by the intended recipients without unwanted interruptions or crosstalk.

Exploring Additional Features

Your Baofeng radio is packed with an array of powerful features that extend far beyond basic communication capabilities. In this section, we will dive into some of the most advanced and innovative functions, unlocking new levels of convenience, efficiency, and versatility in your radio usage.

Voice-Operated Exchange (VOX)

The VOX feature allows you to operate your radio hands-free by using your voice to activate the transmission automatically. This can be incredibly useful in situations where your hands are occupied, such as during outdoor activities or when operating machinery.

To enable VOX, access the relevant menu on your radio and adjust the VOX settings to your desired sensitivity level. Once activated, your radio will transmit whenever it detects your voice, eliminating the need to manually press the PTT (Push-To-Talk) button.

- On channels 1-5, Press and Hold the PTT and MONI buttons while switching ON the transceiver to turn the VOX ON or OFF.

DTMF Capabilities

DTMF (Dual-Tone Multi-Frequency) is a signaling system that uses specific tone combinations to transmit data or commands over radio frequencies. With DTMF capabilities, your Baofeng radio can be used to control external devices, access remote systems, or even activate repeaters that require DTMF tones for access.

To utilize DTMF, you will need to program the appropriate tone sequences into your radio's memory channels or access them through the keypad during transmission. This feature opens up a world of possibilities, allowing you to integrate your radio with various systems and devices for enhanced functionality.

Here is the step-by-step process you have to follow to use DTMF.

NB: If you wait more than 9 seconds between any of these steps, it will automatically go back to the home screen.

1. Press MENU.

2. Press 13 on the keypad (T-CTCS). On this section of the menu, you can edit the tone frequency which will get you into repeaters.

3. Press MENU again to start editing this part of the settings. A menu will appear because you can toggle between all the tone options.

4. Toggle with up/down arrows to the setting you want. You can either press the button repeatedly or press and hold which will turbo-speed you through the frequencies.

5. Press MENU again to save the new settings you have edited in step 4.

6. Press EXIT to get back to the home screen or just wait the 9 seconds and it will return automatically.

Note that you will not see any indication on your home screen that you have a tone on until you transmit. During your first transmission, you will then see a CT lettering appear which means you got the tone saved successfully.

Advanced Scanning Functions

Scanning is a powerful tool that enables your radio to automatically monitor multiple channels or frequencies for activity. Baofeng radios offer advanced scanning features that go beyond basic channel scanning, including options for prioritizing specific channels, scanning multiple bands simultaneously, and even detecting and locking onto active frequencies.

To access these scanning functions, familiarize yourself with the scanning menus and options available on your specific radio model. You can configure scan lists, set priority channels, and customize various scanning parameters to suit your needs. This feature is invaluable for staying informed about active communications across multiple channels or frequencies, ensuring you never miss important transmissions.

Here are some useful functionalities:

Setting up scan lists

1. Access the scan list menu on your radio (refer to your user manual for specific menu navigation).

2. Create a new scan list or select an existing one to edit.

3. Add/remove channels or frequencies to/from the list using the menu options.

4. Set any desired scan parameters, such as scan resume behavior or scan delay times.

Prioritizing channels

1. Within your scan list menu, look for the "Priority Channel" or "Priority Monitoring" option.

2. Select one or more channels you want to be prioritized during scanning.

3. These priority channels will be monitored more frequently than non-prioritized ones.

Multi-band scanning

1. Access the band scope or VFO settings menu.

2. Enable the multi-band scan option if available on your model.

3. Select the desired bands (e.g., VHF, UHF) you want to include in the scan.

4. Start the scan, and your radio will cycle through all selected bands.

Detecting and locking active frequencies

1. Put your radio in VFO mode to allow frequency scanning.

2. Access the scan settings and enable options like "Scan Stop On Active" or similar.

3. Start the scan, and your radio will pause scanning when an active frequency is detected.

4. You can then monitor the active transmission or lock onto that frequency for further use.

Remember, the specific menu options and sequences may vary between different Baofeng models, so always refer to your user manual for accurate instructions. Mastering these advanced scanning functions allows you to stay informed and never miss important transmissions, truly unlocking the full potential of your radio's monitoring capabilities.

USING THE CORRECT LANGUAGE WITH BAOFENG

Effective communication over the radio requires more than just operating the equipment correctly. It also involves adhering to proper radio etiquette and using the correct language. This ensures that transmissions are clear, concise, and easily understood by all parties involved, especially in critical situations where miscommunication could have severe consequences.

Basic Radio Etiquette

- The international radio language is English, except in cases where you are licensed to speak in some other language.
- When using a two-way radio you cannot speak and listen at the same time, as you can with a phone.
- Don't interrupt if you hear other people talking. Wait until their conversation is finished unless it is an emergency. If it is an emergency, inform the other parties that you have an urgent emergency message (refer to the "Emergency Calls" section below).
- Do not respond if you are not sure the call is for you. Wait until you hear your call sign to respond.
- Never transmit sensitive, confidential, financial, or military information. Unless you are certain your conversations are secured with the proper level of encryption for the level of sensitivity, assume your conversations can be heard by others.
- Keep the volume high enough to be able to hear calls.
- Memorize call signs and locations of persons and radio stations you communicate with regularly.
- In radio communication, you are not called by your name. Everybody has their own unique call sign.
- Think before you speak. You have to decide what you are going to say and to whom it is meant.
- Make your conversations as concise, precise, and clear as possible.
- Avoid long and complicated sentences. If your message is long, divide it into separate shorter messages.
- Do not use abbreviations unless they are well understood by your group.

Golden Rules of Radio Use

- **Clarity**: Your voice should be clear. Speak a little slower than normal. Speak in a normal tone, do not shout.
- **Simplicity**: Keep your message simple enough for intended listeners to under-

stand.

- **Brevity**: Be precise and to the point.
- **Security**: Do not transmit confidential information unless you know the proper security technology is in place. Remember, frequencies are shared, you do not have exclusive use of the frequency.

Speaking the Language

In the following table, you will find a list of general terms used to efficiently communicate with your radio.

General Terms	Meaning
Radio Check	What is my signal strength? Can you hear me?
Go ahead	You are ready to receive the transmission.
Stand-by	You acknowledge the other party, but I am unable to respond immediately.
Roger **Ten four**	Message received and understood.
Negative	Same as "No".
Affirmative	Same as "Yes". Avoid "yup" or "nope" as they are difficult to hear.
Say again	Re-transmit your message
Over	Your message is finished.
Out	All conversation is finished, and the channel is clear for others to use.

Break, break, break	You are interrupting in the middle of communication because you have an emergency.
Read you loud and clear **Read you 5-by-5**	Response to "Radio Check". This means your transmission signal is good.
Come in	You are asking the other party to acknowledge they hear you.
Copy	You understand what was said.
Wilco	Means "I will comply".
Repeat	Use before you repeat something. ex: "I require 9-5, repeat 9-5, gallons of diesel fuel. Over"
Sécurité	Safety call. Alert to some safety warnings. Repeat 3 times. Has priority over routine calls.
Pan-pan	Urgent call. Help needed. Repeat 3 times. Has priority over safety calls.
MayDay	Distress call. Repeat 3 times, and again following each transmission. Has priority over all other calls.

Some specific codes were also developed to facilitate communications.

- **10-Codes**: These abbreviations are used to shorten common phrases. They allow for brevity and standardization of messages and have been widely used by law enforcement and in Citizens Band (CB) radio transmissions. Also called 10-signals, they were developed in 1937, and expanded in 1974, by the Association of Public-Safety Communications Officials-International (APCO). They remain in common use but have been phased out in some regions in favor of plain language. Here are some examples:
  - ❖ 10-1 Receiving Poorly
  - ❖ 10-2 Receiving Well
  - ❖ 10-3 Stop Transmitting
  - ❖ 10-4 OK, Message Received

- **Q Codes (ICAO)**: These codes are restricted for aviation services as only stations of the Aeronautical Service will have copies of them.

Radio communication also uses a unique way to spell this alphabet by matching a letter with a word.

A	ALPHA	N	NOVEMBER
B	BRAVO	O	OSCAR
C	CHARLIE	P	PAPA
D	DELTA	Q	QUEBEC
E	ECHO	R	ROMEO
F	FOXTROT	S	SIERRA
G	GOLF	T	TANGO
H	HOTEL	U	UNIFORM
I	INDIA	V	VICTOR
J	JULIET	W	X-RAY
K	KILO	X	WHISKEY
L	LIMA	Y	YANKEE
M	MIKE	Z	ZULU

Making a call

In order to make a call, you can follow these very easy steps.

1. Listen to ensure the channel is clear.
2. Press PUSH-TO-TALK (PTT).
3. Wait for 2 seconds before calling your recipient by his call sign twice, followed by your own call sign.
4. Once you get an answer, you may convey your message.

Here is an example of a radio conversation:

You: "Papa November One, Papa November One, This is Papa November Nine, Come in, Over"   (PN1 is their call sign, PN9 is your call sign)

Recipient: "Papa November Nine, This is Papa November One, Go Ahead, Over"

You: Say your message and then: "Over"

Recipient: "Roger Wilco, Over"

You: "This is Papa November Nine, Over and Out"

As many people may be using the same frequency as you, stating your call sign and one of your correspondents lets everyone know who the message is meant for.

Emergency calls

If you have an emergency message to convey, here is the way to interrupt others' conversations:

1. Listen until you hear "Over".
2. Press PTT and say: "Break, break, break. (Your call sign), I have an emergency message for (recipient's call sign). Do you copy? Over."

ADVANCED TROUBLESHOOTING

As you delve into the advanced features of your Baofeng radio, you may encounter some challenges or issues that require more in-depth troubleshooting. While these advanced functions offer powerful capabilities, they also introduce additional complexities that can lead to potential problems if not properly configured or used correctly.

Repeater Access Difficulties

One common issue that can arise is difficulty in accessing or communicating through repeater systems. If you're experiencing problems with repeater access, here are some steps to troubleshoot:

1. **Double-check your programming**: Ensure that you've entered the correct repeater input and output frequencies, as well as the appropriate offset and shift direction.

2. **Verify CTCSS/DCS settings**: Make sure that your radio's CTCSS or DCS tones match those required by the repeater system you're trying to access.

3. **Check for interference**: Interference from other signals or sources can disrupt repeater communication. Try adjusting your location or antenna position to improve signal quality.

4. **Consult local resources**: Reach out to local radio clubs or repeater system administrators for guidance on proper settings or known issues with specific repeaters.

CTCSS/DCS Interference or Compatibility Issues

If you are experiencing interference or compatibility problems when using CTCSS or DCS codes, consider the following troubleshooting steps:

1. **Verify code settings**: Ensure that all radios in your communication group are using the same CTCSS tone frequency or DCS code and that the codes are set correctly for both transmit and receive functions.

2. **Change codes**: If interference persists, try switching to a different CTCSS tone or DCS code that may be less commonly used in your area.

3. **Check for tone compatibility**: Some older or less advanced radios may not support CTCSS or DCS tones, which can cause compatibility issues. Confirm that all radios in your group are capable of using these features.

Advanced Feature Malfunctions

In some cases, you may encounter issues with advanced features like VOX, DTMF, or advanced scanning functions. If this occurs, try the following troubleshooting steps:

1. **Reset feature settings**: Clear any custom settings or configurations for the malfunctioning feature and try setting it up again from scratch.

2. **Update radio firmware**: Outdated firmware can sometimes cause compatibility issues with advanced features. Check if updates are available for your radio

model and follow the manufacturer's instructions for updating.

3. **Seek expert assistance**: If the issue persists, reach out to the radio manufacturer's technical support or consult with experienced radio technicians or enthusiasts who may have encountered similar problems.

Seeking Further Assistance

If you have exhausted all troubleshooting steps and are still unable to resolve the issue with your advanced features, don't hesitate to seek further assistance. Here are some additional resources you can explore:

1. **Online forums and communities**: Join online radio enthusiast forums or social media groups, where you can post your specific issue and receive advice from experienced users worldwide.

2. **Local radio clubs**: Attend meetings or events hosted by local radio clubs, where you can connect with knowledgeable members who may be able to provide hands-on assistance or guidance.

3. **Professional repair services**: In some cases, your radio may require professional repair or servicing, especially if the issue is hardware-related. Look for authorized repair centers or technicians specializing in Baofeng radios.

Baofeng's customer service email address: support@baofengradio.com

List of Baofeng's authorized dealers: https://baofengtech.com/authorized-distributors/

Remember, advanced features can be powerful tools, but they also require patience, practice, and persistence to master. By following these troubleshooting tips and seeking assistance when needed, you will be better equipped to overcome any challenges and fully harness the capabilities of your Baofeng radio's advanced functions.

Throughout this chapter, we have explored the vast array of advanced features and functionalities offered by Baofeng radios that make them extremely powerful communication devices.

Mastering these advanced operations is crucial to unlocking the full potential of your Baofeng radio and maximizing its capabilities. By taking the time to understand and properly configure these features, you will gain greater control, flexibility, and efficiency in your communication endeavors, ensuring that your radio serves as a versatile and reliable companion in any situation.

Do not be intimidated by the complexity of some of these advanced functions—with practice and perseverance, you will soon become proficient in their use. Embrace the learning curve and be willing to experiment with different settings and configurations until you find the ideal setup that meets your specific needs.

Remember, the journey to becoming a true master of your Baofeng radio is an ongoing process, and there is always more to discover and explore. Engage with the vibrant community of radio enthusiasts, seek guidance from experienced users, and stay updated on the latest advancements and techniques.

So, dive in, experiment, and unlock the full spectrum of possibilities that your Baofeng radio has to offer. With these advanced features at your fingertips, you will be equipped to handle even the most demanding communication challenges, elevating your radio experience to new heights of excellence.

CHAPTER 4: PRACTICAL APPLICATIONS FOR OUTDOOR ENTHUSIASTS

Effective communication can be a matter of safety and enjoyment for outdoor enthusiasts and adventurers. Whatever your plans for adventure, having functional radios is paramount—not only for staying in touch with fellow adventurers but also for coordinating logistics, sharing crucial information, and, most importantly, ensuring safety.

Baofeng radios offer a versatile solution, empowering you to maintain clear communication while navigating the great outdoors. From rugged construction to long-range capabilities, these radios are designed to thrive in the most demanding environments.

In this chapter, we will dive into the practical applications of Baofeng radios for outdoor activities, highlighting their invaluable role. Thanks to your communication device, you will be at peace, knowing that you can immediately call for assistance or relay critical updates in case of emergencies or unexpected situations.

Whether you are an avid hiker, a seasoned climber, or an adrenaline-seeking adventurer, the following section will provide you with the knowledge and insights necessary to harness the full potential of your Baofeng radio, making it a reliable companion on your outdoor excursions.

COMMUNICATION STRATEGIES FOR GROUPS IN THE FIELD

When venturing into the great outdoors with a group, you need to be able to communicate with others to stay safe and coordinated and enjoy your experience. Therefore, establishing clear communication strategies and protocols is essential. With Baofeng radios, you have a powerful tool at your disposal to facilitate seamless communication, even in remote or challenging environments.

Establishing Communication Channels

Before setting off on your outdoor adventure, one of the most crucial steps is to define and establish the communication channels you will be using. This involves selecting specific radio frequencies and potentially utilizing CTCSS/DCS codes to minimize interference and ensure privacy for your group's communications. Taking the time to properly set up your channels will greatly enhance the effectiveness and reliability of your Baofeng radios.

When choosing frequencies for your group, consider the range and purpose of your communication needs. Different frequencies have varying propagation characteristics, which can impact the distance and clarity of your transmissions. Research the frequencies commonly used in the area where you'll be conducting your activities and select those that are appropriate for your specific needs. It's also important to be aware of any local regulations or restrictions regarding the use of certain frequencies.

In addition to selecting frequencies, utilizing CTCSS (Continuous Tone-Coded Squelch System) or DCS (Digital-Coded Squelch) codes can further optimize your communication channels. These codes help to filter out unwanted noise and interference from other radio users who may be operating on the same frequency. By assigning a specific CTCSS or DCS code to your group's channels, you can ensure that only your intended recipients will hear your transmissions.

To program CTCSS/DCS codes into your Baofeng radios, please refer to the detailed instructions provided in the section "Programming CTCSS/DCS codes" in Chapter 3 of this book. This step-by-step guide will walk you through the process of accessing the radio's menu, selecting the desired channel, and assigning the appropriate code. It's essential to follow these instructions carefully and double-check that all group members have programmed the same codes into their radios to ensure seamless communication.

When establishing your communication channels, it's also a good idea to designate specific channels for different purposes. For example, you may assign one channel for general group communication, another for emergency situations, and perhaps a third for specific subgroups or activities. By having clearly defined channels, you can minimize confusion and ensure that important messages are transmitted on the appropriate channel.

Once you have selected your frequencies and programmed any necessary CTCSS/DCS codes, be sure to test your radios before heading out. Conduct a brief communication check to ensure that all group members can send and receive transmissions clearly on the designated channels. This will give you peace of mind knowing that your radios are properly set up and ready for use in the field.

It's also important to familiarize yourself and your group with proper radio etiquette and communication protocols. Establish guidelines for speaking clearly and concisely, using appropriate language, and allowing for breaks between transmissions to avoid overlapping. By setting these expectations upfront, you can ensure that your group communicates effectively and efficiently throughout your outdoor adventure.

Assigning Roles and Responsibilities

To ensure efficient information flow and maintain clear communication throughout your outdoor activities, it's highly recommended to assign specific roles and responsibilities related to radio communication. By clearly defining these roles and expectations, you can create a more organized and effective communication structure within your group.

One key role to consider is that of a communication lead or coordinator. This individual would be responsible for managing radio traffic, prioritizing transmissions, and maintaining situational awareness. The communication lead should have a strong understanding of your group's communication protocols, frequencies, and equipment, as well as the ability to make quick decisions and keep the group informed and organized.

Some specific responsibilities of the communication lead may include:

1. Monitoring the designated channels and frequencies to ensure they remain clear and available for use.

2. Coordinating regular check-ins and status updates from group members.

3. Prioritizing and directing radio traffic based on urgency and relevance.

4. Relaying important information, such as weather updates, route changes, or emergency alerts, to the entire group.

5. Maintaining a log of important transmissions and decisions for reference and debriefing purposes.

In addition to the communication lead, it's a good idea to assign backup communicators within your group. These individuals can step in to assist the lead or take over communication responsibilities if needed, such as during rest breaks or in the event that the primary lead becomes unavailable. Having multiple people familiar with the communication protocols and equipment ensures that your group can maintain consistent communication at all times.

When assigning roles, consider the skills, experience, and comfort level of each group member using the Baofeng radios and communication protocols. It may be beneficial to rotate roles and responsibilities throughout your outdoor activity to provide opportunities for everyone to gain experience and to prevent fatigue or burnout for those in key communication positions.

Before embarking on your adventure, take the time to clearly communicate the assigned roles and responsibilities to all group members. Ensure that everyone understands their specific duties and how they contribute to the overall communication strategy. Provide necessary training or practice sessions to familiarize individuals with their roles and the equipment they will be using.

It's also important to establish a chain of command or hierarchy for communication decision-making. In the event of conflicting information or priorities, having a clear understanding of who has the authority to make final decisions can help avoid confusion and maintain order.

Throughout your outdoor activity, encourage open communication and feedback among group members regarding the effectiveness of the assigned roles and responsibilities. Be prepared to make adjustments as needed based on the group's experiences and changing circumstances.

Radio Etiquette and Protocols

As stated in Chapter 3, respecting radio etiquette and transmission protocols is essential for maintaining order and clarity in your communications. By following established guidelines and best practices, you can ensure that your group's radio communications are efficient, effective, and professional.

When initiating a transmission, it's important to follow a clear and consistent protocol. This may include using a specific call sign or identifier to address the intended recipient, such as "Base Camp, this is Team Alpha, over." By using predetermined call signs, you can quickly and clearly establish who is speaking and to whom the message is directed.

Before beginning your transmission, take a moment to listen to the channel and ensure that it is clear and available. Avoid interrupting ongoing conversations or transmissions unless it is an emergency. When you have confirmed that the channel is free, proceed with your message.

When speaking, it's crucial to adhere to any predefined message structures or formats that your group has established. This may include starting with a clear indication of the message's priority or urgency, followed by the main content of the transmission. For example, "Priority one message: We have reached checkpoint Alpha and are proceeding to checkpoint Bravo, over."

Keep your transmissions concise and to the point. Avoid unnecessary chatter or irrelevant information that may clutter the channel and distract from important messages. Focus on conveying essential details and instructions clearly and efficiently.

After completing your transmission, end with a clear indication that you are finished speaking and await a response, such as "Over" or "Out." This signals to other group members that the channel is now available for them to respond to or initiate their own transmissions.

As important as speaking clearly is actively listening to the channel for important updates, instructions, or requests from other group members. Maintain situational awareness and be prepared to respond promptly and appropriately to any communications directed towards you or your subgroup.

In addition to these basic protocols, there are a few other considerations to keep in mind:

1. Avoid using profanity, offensive language, or inappropriate humor on the radio. Keep your communications professional and respectful.

2. If you need to convey sensitive or confidential information, consider using pre-determined code words or phrases to maintain privacy.

3. In the event of an emergency or urgent situation, follow your group's established emergency communication protocols, which may include using specific emergency channels or codes.

4. Be mindful of your radio's battery life and carry spare batteries or a means to recharge them as needed. Regularly check your battery status and inform your group if you anticipate any communication limitations due to low battery power.

Coordinating Activities and Updates

Baofeng radios provide an excellent platform for coordinating group activities and sharing real-time updates. By using designated channels, you can effectively relay information about planned routes, rest stops, or changes in the itinerary. This ensures that everyone in your group stays informed and on the same page throughout your outdoor adventure. To make the most of your Baofeng radios for coordination, consider assigning specific roles and responsibilities to group members. For example, designate a lead communicator who is responsible for initiating check-ins and relaying important updates. This person can also serve as a central point of contact for any questions or concerns that arise during the activity.

Encourage each member of your group to regularly report on their location, progress, or any notable conditions they encounter. This can include sharing information about trail conditions, weather changes, or potential hazards. By maintaining open lines of communication, you can quickly adapt to changing circumstances and make informed decisions as a group.

When coordinating activities, it's important to establish clear communication protocols to avoid confusion or overlapping transmissions. Develop a system for taking turns speaking, such as using the word "over" to indicate when a transmission is complete. Additionally, agree on specific terminology or codes for different situations, such as "all clear" to indicate that a member has safely reached a designated checkpoint.

Baofeng radios also offer the flexibility to create subgroups or separate channels for specific purposes. For instance, if your group is splitting up to explore different areas or engage in separate activities, you can assign different channels to each subgroup.

This allows for targeted communication within each team while still maintaining the ability to switch back to the main channel for overall coordination.

In addition to verbal communication, Baofeng radios can be used to transmit important data or information. Some models feature the ability to send text messages or share GPS coordinates, which can be valuable for providing precise location updates or relaying detailed instructions. Familiarize yourself with these advanced features and incorporate them into your coordination strategies as needed.

When planning your outdoor activities, take into account the range and limitations of your Baofeng radios. Be aware of potential obstacles, such as mountains or dense foliage, that may impact signal strength. If you anticipate challenges in maintaining consistent communication, consider establishing predetermined checkpoints or rendezvous points where group members can reconnect and share updates.

It's also crucial to have backup plans in case of communication failures or emergencies. Ensure that all group members are familiar with alternative communication methods, such as using whistles or visual signals, in case radio communication becomes impossible. Regularly review and practice these backup plans to ensure a smooth and coordinated response in any situation.

Emergency Response and Coordination

In the event of an emergency or unexpected situation, having a well-established communication strategy can be life-saving. Baofeng radios play a crucial role in facilitating effective emergency response and coordination during outdoor activities. By implementing clear protocols and leveraging the capabilities of these radios, you can ensure a swift and organized response when it matters most.

Before embarking on your adventure, take the time to determine specific protocols for initiating emergency transmissions. Assign a dedicated emergency channel or frequency that all group members are aware of and can quickly switch to in case of a crisis. Establish a clear and concise format for relaying crucial information, such as the nature of the emergency, the location of those involved, and any immediate assistance required.

It's essential to ensure that all group members understand the procedures for responding to emergencies. Conduct a thorough briefing before your activity, outlining the steps to be taken in various scenarios. This may include designating rally points where the group can safely gather and assess the situation, as well as discussing evacuation plans or procedures for contacting emergency services.

During an emergency, the ability to relay accurate and timely information is paramount. Encourage group members to remain calm and speak clearly when transmitting messages. Use simple and standardized language to avoid confusion and ensure that critical details are effectively communicated. If possible, have one designated person responsible for communicating with emergency responders to maintain clarity and consistency.

In addition to verbal communication, Baofeng radios can be used to transmit vital data that can aid in emergency response. Some models allow for the transmission of GPS coordinates, which can be invaluable in providing precise location information to rescue teams. Familiarize yourself with these features and include them in your emergency response protocols.

It's also crucial to regularly practice and review your emergency communication procedures. Conduct drills or simulations to familiarize group members with the protocols and identify any areas for improvement. Ensure that everyone knows how to operate the radios effectively under stress and can quickly access emergency channels or frequencies.

When faced with an emergency, it's important to prioritize the safety and well-being of all group members. Use your Baofeng radios to maintain contact with each other, provide updates on the situation, and coordinate any necessary actions. If the emergency requires outside assistance, be prepared to provide clear and concise information to emergency responders, including your location, the nature of the incident, and any specific needs or hazards.

Remember that effective emergency response relies on a combination of preparedness, clear communication, and swift action. By taking the time to establish robust emergency protocols and familiarizing yourself with the capabilities of your Baofeng radios, you can greatly enhance your ability to handle unexpected situations and ensure the safety of your group.

Enhancing Safety During Outdoor Activities

While outdoor activities offer exhilarating experiences and a chance to connect with nature, they also come with inherent risks. Fortunately, Baofeng radios can play a crucial role in enhancing safety and preparedness during your adventures. By incorporating proper communication strategies and leveraging the features of these radios, you can mitigate potential dangers and respond effectively to emergencies.

One of the key benefits of using Baofeng radios during outdoor activities is the ability to maintain constant communication with your group members or a designated base camp. Whether you're hiking through remote trails, camping in the wilderness, or engaging in extreme sports, staying connected is essential for coordinating movements, sharing important information, and ensuring everyone's well-being. With

Baofeng radios, you can establish reliable communication channels, even in areas where cellular coverage is limited or nonexistent.

Before leaving for your outdoor adventure, it's crucial to familiarize yourself with the features and functions of your Baofeng radio. Take the time to program essential frequencies, such as those used by local emergency services or designated group channels. Ensure that all members of your group are proficient in operating the radios and understand the proper communication protocols.

In addition to maintaining group communication, Baofeng radios can be invaluable for receiving weather updates and emergency alerts. Many models come equipped with NOAA weather radio channels, allowing you to stay informed about changing weather conditions, severe storms, or other potential hazards in your area. By monitoring these channels regularly, you can make informed decisions about altering your plans or seeking shelter when necessary.

Another critical aspect of enhancing safety with Baofeng radios is having a well-defined emergency communication plan. Before setting out, designate specific frequencies or channels for emergencies and ensure that everyone in your group is aware of them. In the event of an accident, injury, or other crisis, having a clear protocol for contacting help can make a significant difference in the outcome. Consider programming emergency frequencies into your radio's memory for quick access and regularly practice emergency communication drills to build confidence and familiarity.

To further optimize the safety benefits of Baofeng radios, consider investing in additional accessories and features. For example, some models offer GPS functionality, allowing you to share your location with others or access navigation assistance. Waterproof or water-resistant radios can provide added protection in wet or humid environments, while long-range antennas can extend your communication reach in vast or challenging terrains.

Emergency Preparedness and Response

Integrating Baofeng radios into your emergency preparedness plan can significantly improve your ability to handle unexpected situations in the great outdoors. You must establish protocols for sending distress signals or SOS transmissions, ensuring that all group members understand the specific codes or procedures to follow.

Additionally, you may consider implementing a check-in system, where group members are required to report their status and location at predetermined intervals. This practice can help detect and respond to potential issues promptly, minimizing the risk of escalation.

In case of an emergency, your Baofeng radio can be the key element for coordinating rescue efforts or requesting assistance from emergency services. Make sure that you have the necessary contact information or frequencies for local search and rescue teams, park rangers, or other relevant authorities programmed into your radio for quick access.

Here are two websites where you can find them:

- https://www.fcc.gov/
- https://www.radioreference.com/

WEATHER MONITORING AND ADAPTATION

Sudden weather changes can pose significant risks during outdoor activities, making effective communication essential for staying informed and adapting to the conditions. You can use your Baofeng radio to monitor weather reports or alerts from relevant sources and share crucial information with your group members.

If severe weather is approaching, your radio can facilitate coordinated decision-making, such as seeking shelter, adjusting routes, or initiating evacuation procedures. Clear communication can help prevent individuals from becoming separated or stranded in hazardous conditions.

Your Baofeng radio can serve as a valuable tool for monitoring weather conditions, especially in remote or off-grid areas where traditional weather reporting services may be unavailable or unreliable. By tuning into specific frequencies dedicated to weather broadcasts, you can stay informed about potential storms, severe weather events, and changing weather patterns, allowing you to make informed decisions and take necessary precautions.

Accessing Weather Radio Frequencies

To receive weather information on your Baofeng radio, you will need to program the appropriate frequencies used for weather broadcasts in your area. These frequencies are typically in the VHF band and are operated by national or regional weather services.

In the United States, the National Oceanic and Atmospheric Administration (NOAA) operates a network of weather radio stations that broadcast continuous weather information, including forecasts, warnings, and emergency alerts. The primary frequencies used by NOAA Weather Radio are:

- 162.400 MHz
- 162.425 MHz
- 162.450 MHz
- 162.475 MHz
- 162.500 MHz
- 162.525 MHz
- 162.550 MHz

In other countries, weather radio frequencies may vary, so it's essential to research and program the appropriate frequencies for your location.

Here are some resources to find weather radio frequencies worldwide:

- radioreference.com
  - ❖ This website has a comprehensive database of radio frequencies, including weather radio frequencies for various countries and regions.
  - ❖ You can search by location or browse by country/region to find the relevant weather radio frequencies.

- National Weather Service Websites
  - ❖ Many national weather services provide lists of their weather radio frequencies on their official websites.
  - ❖ For example, the US National Weather Service has a list of NOAA Weather Radio frequencies by state: https://www.weather.gov/nwr/station_listings

- International Maritime Organization (IMO) Publications
  - ❖ The IMO publishes the "List of Radio Signals" which includes weather radio frequencies used by various countries for maritime purposes.
  - ❖ This publication is updated periodically and can be purchased or accessed through some online resources.

- World Meteorological Organization (WMO)
  - ❖ The WMO is a specialized agency of the United Nations for meteorology. They maintain information on weather radio frequencies used by member

countries.

- ❖ You may need to contact the WMO or check their publications for specific frequency details.

- Environment Canada
  - ❖ Provides weather radio frequencies for Canada.
  - ❖ https://www.canada.ca/en/environment-climate-change/services/weatheradio/find-your-network.html

Programming Weather Radio Frequencies

To program weather radio frequencies into your Baofeng radio, follow these steps:

1. Access the frequency programming menu on your radio.

2. Select the desired frequency band (typically VHF) and enter the appropriate weather radio frequency for your area.

3. Save the frequency to a dedicated memory channel or channel group for easy access.

4. Repeat the process for additional weather radio frequencies you wish to monitor.

Monitoring Weather Broadcasts

Once you have programmed the weather radio frequencies into your Baofeng radio, you can monitor weather broadcasts by switching to the designated memory channels or channel group. It is recommended to periodically check these channels for updates, especially when planning outdoor activities or before embarking on trips to remote areas.

While monitoring weather broadcasts, be attentive to any severe weather warnings or emergency alerts issued by the weather service. These alerts may include information about potential storms, hurricanes, tornadoes, or other extreme weather events, as well as instructions on how to seek shelter or evacuate if necessary.

Wildlife Encounters

Encounters with wildlife or navigation challenges are common occurrences in the great outdoors, and Baofeng radios can play a vital role in addressing these situations safely. If you encounter potentially dangerous wildlife, use your radio to alert your group members, coordinate a safe retreat, or request assistance if necessary.

Similarly, if you find yourself lost or disoriented, your radio can be a lifeline for communicating your location, sharing navigational information, and coordinating with others to find your way back to safety.

As already mentioned, incorporating Baofeng radios into your safety protocols and emergency preparedness plans can significantly enhance your ability to respond to various situations and mitigate risks. Effective communication and collaboration among group members can make the difference between a minor setback and a potentially life-threatening scenario.

Remember, safety should always be a top priority when engaging in outdoor activities. Leveraging the capabilities of your radio device and implementing proper communication strategies will enable you to enjoy your adventures with greater peace of mind and confidence.

Navigation Challenges

While Baofeng radios are primarily designed for communication purposes, they can also serve as valuable tools for navigation, especially in off-grid or remote scenarios. By harnessing the features of your Baofeng radio and combining them with basic navigation techniques, you can increase your chances of finding your way back to safety and civilization.

Using Radio Direction Finding (RDF)

One of the most useful navigation techniques with Baofeng radios is Radio Direction Finding (RDF), also known as fox hunting or radio orienteering. This technique involves using your radio's signal strength indicator to determine the direction of a known transmitter or beacon, which can guide you toward a specific location or back to a familiar area.

To use RDF with your Baofeng radio, you will need to have programmed a specific frequency or channel that is being transmitted from a known location, such as a base camp, trailhead, or emergency beacon. By rotating your radio and observing the signal strength indicator, you can identify the direction from which the signal is strongest, and use that information to navigate towards the transmitter.

Note that RDF can be affected by various factors, such as terrain, obstacles, and interference. Therefore, we advise you to practice this technique in controlled environments before relying on it in critical situations.

Triangulation with Multiple Transmitters

Another navigation technique that can be employed with Baofeng radios is triangulation. This method involves using two or more known transmitter locations to determine your approximate position by measuring the signal strength of each transmitter.

To use triangulation, you will need to have programmed the frequencies or channels of at least two known transmitters in your area. By measuring signal strength and direction measurements from each of them and plotting them on a map, you can estimate your location based on the intersection of the lines.

Triangulation can be a more accurate navigation method than RDF, but it requires knowledge of the transmitter locations and may be more complex to implement in the field.

Emergency Locator Beacons and SOS Features

In addition to navigation techniques, many Baofeng radios also offer emergency locator beacons and SOS features. They can aid in rescue efforts if you find yourself in a critical situation by transmitting a distress signal on a dedicated frequency or channel. This signal can be picked up by search and rescue teams or other radio operators in the area, allowing them to pinpoint your location and coordinate rescue efforts. Some of these devices may also convey your GPS coordinates or other location information.

To activate the emergency locator beacon or SOS feature on your Baofeng radio, consult your user manual for the specific steps or button combinations. It is crucial to familiarize yourself with this feature and its activation process before embarking on any off-grid or remote adventures, as every second counts in an emergency situation.

By understanding how to activate the emergency locator beacon or SOS feature on your Baofeng radio, you can increase your chances of being located and rescued in critical situations when traditional communication methods are unavailable or ineffective.

Combining Radio Navigation with Traditional Techniques

While Baofeng radios can provide valuable navigation assistance, it is important to combine these techniques with traditional navigation methods, such as map reading, compass navigation, and landmark recognition. By integrating radio navigation with these skills, you can create a more robust and reliable navigation strategy, increasing your chances of finding your way back to safety.

Remember, navigation in off-grid or remote areas can be challenging, and it is always advisable to have a backup plan, carry essential survival gear, and inform others of your intended route and estimated return time. By leveraging the capabilities of your

Baofeng radio and developing robust navigation skills, you can enhance your preparedness and confidence when venturing into the great outdoors.

CASE STUDIES AND REAL-LIFE EXAMPLES

While the theoretical applications of Baofeng radios for outdoor enthusiasts are invaluable, nothing reinforces their practical utility more than real-life examples and case studies. Examining successful communication strategies and their impact in real-world scenarios gives us a deeper appreciation for the critical role these radios play in ensuring safety, coordination, and positive outcomes during outdoor adventures.

Coordinating a Successful Rescue Operation

In the rugged wilderness of the Rocky Mountains, a group of experienced hikers found themselves in a precarious situation when one of their members sustained a serious injury after a fall. With no cell phone reception and the nearest trailhead miles away, the group relied on their Baofeng radios to coordinate a rescue operation.

By establishing clear communication protocols and assigning specific roles, the group was able to provide accurate updates on the injured hiker's condition, relay their precise location, and request emergency assistance from local search and rescue teams. Through effective radio communication, the rescue teams were able to swiftly locate the group and evacuate the injured hiker to a nearby medical facility, potentially saving their life.

Providing Crucial First Aid Assistance

During a challenging rock-climbing expedition in the Sierra Nevada range, a climber suffered a severe laceration from a falling rock. While the group had basic first aid training, they were unsure how to properly treat the injury and minimize blood loss.

Fortunately, one of the climbers had the foresight to program the frequency of a nearby ranger station into their Baofeng radio. They were able to establish communication with the rangers, who provided step-by-step instructions for administering first aid and stabilizing the injured climber until a rescue team could arrive.

Navigating Challenging Terrain and Adverse Weather

A group of seasoned backpackers embarked on an ambitious multi-day trek through the Appalachian Trail. Unfortunately, they ended up facing unexpected challenges when a sudden storm system brought heavy rain, strong winds, and reduced visibility. As their planned route became treacherous and the risk of getting lost increased, the group relied on their Baofeng radios to stay connected and navigate the challenging terrain safely.

By maintaining constant communication and sharing their respective locations, the group was able to adjust their itinerary, find suitable shelter, and eventually regroup once the storm passed. Their effective use of radios ensured that no one was separated or stranded, allowing them to complete their trek without any serious incidents.

Lessons Learned and Best Practices

These real-life examples highlight the invaluable role that Baofeng radios can play in outdoor adventures, serving as a lifeline in emergency situations, facilitating crucial communication, and enabling effective coordination among group members.

From these case studies, we can derive several key lessons and best practices:

Establish clear communication protocols and assign roles within your group before embarking on your adventure.

Program essential frequencies, such as those for emergency services or local authorities, into your radios for quick access.

Regularly practice and test your communication strategies to ensure familiarity and preparedness.

Maintain situational awareness and share relevant updates, such as changes in weather or terrain conditions, with your group.

Prioritize safety and be willing to adapt your plans based on the information and coordination facilitated by your radio communication.

By applying these lessons and best practices, outdoor enthusiasts can harness the full potential of their Baofeng radios, enhancing their safety, preparedness, and overall enjoyment of their adventures in the great outdoors.

ADVANCED GEAR INTEGRATION

While Baofeng radios are incredibly versatile and powerful communication tools on their own, integrating them with other outdoor gear and equipment can further enhance their functionality and convenience in the field. Combining these radios with compatible accessories and complementary gear helps outdoor enthusiasts optimize their communication capabilities, tailoring them to the unique demands of their adventures.

Compatible Accessories

Baofeng offers a wide range of accessories designed to improve the performance and usability of their radios in outdoor settings. Here are three additional elements we advise you to consider:

High-quality headsets or earpieces: Enables hands-free operation and clear audio reception, even in noisy or windy environments. Look for ruggedized models with noise-canceling features and a secure, comfortable fit for extended use.

External antenna: Significantly boosts the radio's range and signal strength, ensuring reliable communication even in areas with obstructions or challenging terrain. Compact, flexible antennas that can be easily packed and deployed are ideal for outdoor enthusiasts on the move.

Advanced microphones: Feature noise-canceling capabilities or weather-resistant designs and can be a worthwhile investment for outdoor adventures. These microphones can improve audio clarity and reduce interference from environmental factors like wind or rain, ensuring your transmissions are crystal clear.

Gear Integration

In addition to dedicated accessories, outdoor enthusiasts can explore integrating their Baofeng radios with other outdoor gear and equipment for enhanced convenience and functionality. For example, many modern backpacks and hiking apparel feature built-in pockets or attachment points specifically designed to securely carry radios, allowing for easy access and minimizing the risk of loss or damage.

For outdoor activities that require the use of helmets, such as rock climbing or cycling, radio-compatible helmet mounts or integrated communication systems can be invaluable. These solutions enable you to keep your hands free while maintaining constant communication with your group or receiving important updates.

Power solutions are another consideration for extended outdoor excursions. Portable solar chargers or high-capacity external battery packs can ensure that your Baofeng radio remains operational, even when traditional power sources are unavailable.

Selecting the Right Gear

When selecting accessories and outdoor gear to integrate with your Baofeng radio, it's important to consider factors such as durability, weatherproofing, and compatibility. Look for products designed specifically for outdoor use, with ruggedized construction and water-resistant or waterproof ratings.

Also, make sure that the accessories you choose are compatible with your specific Baofeng radio model and conform to any relevant regulations or standards. Discussions with experienced outdoor enthusiasts or radio experts can provide valuable insights into the most reliable and capable gear for your needs.

Thoughtfully integrating your Baofeng radio with the right accessories and outdoor gear can help you create a highly capable and convenient communication system tailored to your specific outdoor activities. This advanced gear integration not only enhances your radio's performance but also contributes to a more seamless and enjoyable experience in the great outdoors.

Throughout this chapter, we have explored the invaluable role that Baofeng radios can play in enhancing the safety, coordination, and overall experience of outdoor adventures. From establishing effective communication strategies for groups to leveraging advanced gear integration, these radios offer a powerful tool for navigating the challenges and embracing the joys of the great outdoors.

As outdoor enthusiasts ourselves, we understand the thrill of exploration and the importance of being prepared for any situation that may arise. Incorporating the strategies and insights discussed in this chapter allows you to elevate your outdoor experiences to new heights, ensuring that every adventure is not only exhilarating but also secure and well-coordinated.

Embrace the power of communication by implementing clear protocols, assigning roles, and fostering a culture of situational awareness within your group. Utilize your Baofeng radios as a lifeline for coordinating emergency responses, sharing crucial updates, and adapting to changing conditions seamlessly.

Remember, the real-life examples and case studies presented serve as powerful reminders of the positive impact effective communication can have in overcoming challenges and potentially life-threatening situations. Draw inspiration from these stories and apply the lessons learned to your outdoor pursuits, ensuring that you and your companions are equipped with the knowledge and tools to navigate even the most demanding environments safely.

Moreover, feel free to explore advanced gear integration opportunities, combining your Baofeng radio with compatible accessories and outdoor equipment. This strategic integration can optimize performance, enhance convenience, and create a truly seamless communication experience tailored to your specific needs.

As you venture forth into the great outdoors, carry with you the confidence that comes from having a reliable and versatile communication tool at your disposal. Embrace the adventure, but do so with the peace of mind that effective communication and preparation can provide.

Remember, the true essence of outdoor exploration lies in the journey itself, and with the insights and strategies from this chapter, you can embark on that journey with greater assurance, safety, and the ability to create lasting memories in the embrace of nature.

CHAPTER 5: TACTICAL USES FOR LAW ENFORCEMENT AND MILITARY

Law enforcement and military operations require effective communication to transmit and receive information clearly and securely. Successful mission execution and the safety of personnel are dependent on reliable and robust communication systems in these high-stakes environments.

Radios play a vital role in facilitating communication during tactical operations. They enable law enforcement and military personnel to coordinate their actions, share situational awareness, and maintain command and control. However, as the real-life examples and case studies presented earlier in this guide demonstrate, the capacity to communicate effectively in challenging situations is not a guarantee.

This chapter focuses on the tactical uses of radios, specifically those used by law enforcement and military personnel. Secure and effective communication systems are important in high-stakes environments where lives and operational success depend on the ability to transmit and receive information clearly and reliably.

These radios must be durable and capable of enduring the demands of the environments they're used in. They must also offer secure communication capabilities to ensure that information is transmitted securely and cannot be intercepted or compromised.

Law enforcement and military operations require secure and reliable communication systems that can operate in even the most challenging environments, as highlighted in this chapter. Users can better appreciate the vital role radios play in ensuring successful mission execution and the safety of personnel by understanding the tactical applications of radios.

COORDINATION DURING OPERATIONS

In high-stakes law enforcement and military operations, coordination, awareness of the situation, and the accomplishment of tactical goals all depend on effective communication. These environments require robust communication protocols, clear hierarchies, and secure channels to facilitate seamless information exchange among personnel.

Establishing Communication Hierarchies

During tactical operations, establishing a clear hierarchy of communication is crucial for preserving control and facilitating effective communication. Higher-ranking officers or leaders are at the top of this hierarchy, and subordinate units or teams are below them.

Different units or teams can communicate internally while also allowing for cross-unit communication, when necessary, by assigning specific channels or frequencies within this hierarchy. Furthermore, command and control channels are often reserved for higher-level coordination and decision-making.

Implementing Codewords and Signals

Codewords, signals, or encrypted communication systems are used to enhance operational security and prevent information from being intercepted or compromised. It is important that sensitive information is transmitted securely and cannot be easily deciphered by unauthorized parties.

Codewords may be used to convey specific instructions, locations, or tactical maneuvers without revealing their true meaning to anyone intercepting the communication. Critical information can be relayed quickly and discreetly when stealth is required or during high-risk situations by using predetermined signals or codes.

Here are the general ten codes used by law enforcement and emergency services and their meanings.

10-1	Unable to Copy - Change Location	10-18	Quickly	10-35	Major Crime Alert
10-2	Signal Good	10-19	Return to _ _ _	10-36	Correct Time
10-3	Stop Transmitting	10-20	Location	10-37	(Investigate) Suspicious Vehicle
10-4	Acknowledgment (OK)	10-21	Call (_ _) by Phone	10-38	Stopping Suspicious Vehicle
10-5	Relay	10-22	Disregard	10-39	Urgent-Use Light, Siren
10-6	Busy-Unless Urgent	10-23	Arrived at Scene	10-40	Silent Run-No Light, Siren
10-7	Out of Service	10-24	Assignment Completed	10-41	Beginning Tour of Duty
10-8	In Service	10-25	Report in Person (Meet)	10-42	Ending Tour of Duty

10-9	Repeat	**10-26**	Detaining Subject, Expedite	**10-43**	Information
10-10	Fight in Progress	**10-27**	(Driver) License Information	**10-44**	Permission to Leave _ _ for _ _
10-11	Dog Case	**10-28**	Vehicle Registration Information	**10-45**	Animal Carcass at _ _
10-12	Stand By (Stop)	**10-29**	Check for Wanted	**10-46**	Assist Motorist
10-13	Weather-Road Report	**10-30**	Unnecessary Use of Radio	**10-47**	Emergency Road Repair at _ _
10-14	Prowler Report	**10-31**	Crime in Progress	**10-48**	Traffic Standard Repair at _ _
10-15	Civil Disturbance	**10-32**	Man with Gun	**10-49**	Traffic Light Out at _ _
10-16	Domestic Problem	**10-33**	Emergency	**10-50**	Accident (F, PI, PD)(1)
10-17	Meet Complainant	**10-34**	Riot	**10-51**	Wrecker Needed

10-52	Ambulance Needed	**10-69**	Message Received	**10-86**	Officer / Operator on Duty
10-53	Road Blocked at _ _	**10-70**	Fire Alarm	**10-87**	Pickup / Distribute Checks
10-54	Livestock on Highway	**10-71**	Advise Nature of Fire	**10-88**	Present Telephone # of _ _
10-55	Intoxicated Driver	**10-72**	Report progress on Fire	**10-89**	Bomb Threat
10-56	Intoxicated Pedestrian	**10-73**	Smoke Report	**10-90**	Bank Alarm at _ _
10-57	Hit and Run (F, PI, PD)[1]	**10-74**	Negative	**10-91**	Pick Up Prisoner / Subject
10-58	Direct Traffic	**10-75**	In Contact with _ _	**10-92**	Improperly Parked Vehicle
10-59	Convoy or Escort	**10-76**	En Route _ _	**10-93**	Blockade
10-60	Squad in Vicinity	**10-77**	ETA (Estimated Time of Arrival)	**10-94**	Drag Racing

10-61	Personnel in Area	**10-78**	Need Assistance	**10-95**	Prisoner / Subject in Custody
10-62	Reply to Message	**10-79**	Notify Coroner	**10-96**	Mental Subject
10-63	Prepare to Make Written Copy	**10-80**	Chase in Progress	**10-97**	Check (Test) Signal
10-64	Message for Local Delivery	**10-81**	Breathalyzer Report	**10-98**	Prison / Jail Break
10-65	Net Message Assignment	**10-82**	Reserve Lodging	**10-99**	Wanted / Stolen Indicated
10-66	Message Cancellation	**10-83**	Work School Crossing at _	**10-101**	What is Status?
10-67	Clear for Net Message	**10-84**	If Meeting _ _ Advise ETA	**10-106**	Status is secure
10-68	Dispatch Information	**10-85**	Delay Due to _ _	**¹ F – Fire, PI – Personal Injury, PD – Property Damage**	

Case Study: Reconnaissance Mission

Communication skills were crucial for a successful reconnaissance mission in hostile territory. Multiple teams were tasked with collecting intelligence on enemy positions and movements.

To facilitate coordination, a clear communication hierarchy was established, with the mission commander overseeing all operations and individual team leaders managing their respective units. Each team was assigned dedicated channels, which allowed them to communicate internally and report their findings directly to the mission commander.

Furthermore, a set of codewords and signals was developed to convey sensitive information securely. For instance, the codeword "Falcon" was used to indicate the presence of enemy forces, while specific numerical codes were used to report the number and types of enemy assets observed.

The mission commander was able to make informed decisions and adjust the operational plan as needed by adhering to these communication protocols. This level of coordination and secure communication was essential in ensuring the mission's success and the safe extraction of all personnel.

Case Study: Special Operations Assault

During a high-risk special operations assault on an enemy compound, effective communication was critical for coordinating the various elements involved and ensuring the safety of the assault team.

A dedicated command and control channel was established, with the operations commander overseeing the entire operation from a secure location. A dedicated command and control channel was established, with the operation's commander overseeing the entire operation from a secure location. Individual team leaders were assigned separate channels to communicate with their respective teams, which enabled them to coordinate their movements and actions without cluttering the command channel.

The teams were able to share sensitive information without revealing their true intentions or positions thanks to a comprehensive collection of codewords and signals developed to safeguard their operations. The codeword "Thunderstorm" was used to signal the initiation of the assault, while specific numerical codes were used to report casualties or indicate the need for additional support.

Air support, medical evacuation teams, and reinforcements were all coordinated through the command-and-control channel throughout the mission. The secure communication protocols prevented the enemy from gaining any intelligence about the operation, minimizing the risk of compromise or ambush.

These case studies highlight the critical importance of effective communication in law enforcement and military operations. This is achieved by establishing clear communication hierarchies, implementing secure protocols, and fostering coordination among various units.

INTEGRATING BAOFENG RADIOS WITH OTHER COMMUNICATION SYSTEMS

In modern law enforcement and military operations, communication systems are often intricate and multifaceted, involving a variety of devices and networks. Integration of Baofeng radios with existing communication infrastructures and systems is essential to ensure seamless coordination and information exchange.

Interoperability Solutions

Incorporating Baofeng radios with other communication equipment is a key consideration for law enforcement agencies and military units. This can involve integrating them with handheld radios from different manufacturers, vehicle-mounted communication systems, and command center infrastructure.

Cross-band repeaters or gateways enable the translation and retransmission of signals between different frequency bands or communication protocols. These devices can help bridge the gap between Baofeng radios operating on specific frequencies and other systems operating on different bands or using proprietary protocols.

Furthermore, software-based interoperability solutions can be employed to facilitate communication between Baofeng radios and digital communication networks. These solutions often involve the use of software and hardware interfaces that translate and route data between different systems.

Interfacing with Digital Networks and Encrypted Channels

Secure and reliable communication is a priority in many tactical scenarios These requirements can be met by configuring Baofeng radios to connect to digital communication networks, satellite communication networks, and encrypted channels.

Baofeng radios can be integrated with existing digital communication infrastructures by leveraging appropriate hardware and software solutions, enabling personnel to transmit and receive data, voice, and multimedia content securely and efficiently.

Furthermore, Baofeng radios can be equipped with encryption capabilities, allowing for secure communication over encrypted channels. This is particularly important in situations where sensitive information needs to be transmitted without the risk of interception or compromise.

Configuration Tips

Proper configuration is crucial for integrating Baofeng radios with existing communication systems. Here are some tips for ensuring a seamless integration :

1. Consult with communication specialists or system administrators to understand the specific requirements and protocols of the existing infrastructure.

2. Get and configure any necessary hardware or software interfaces, such as cross-band repeaters, gateways, or encryption modules.

3. To ensure compatibility with the integrated systems, program the appropriate frequencies, channels, and encryption keys into the Baofeng radios to ensure compatibility.

4. To identify and address any potential issues or compatibility conflicts, test the integration thoroughly, simulating various operational scenarios to identify and address any potential issues.

5. Provide comprehensive training to personnel on the proper use and configuration of the integrated communication systems, ensuring they are proficient in their operation.

By successfully integrating Baofeng radios with other communication systems, law enforcement agencies, and military units can take advantage of these affordable and versatile radios while ensuring seamless connectivity, enhanced situational awareness, and secure communication during tactical operations.

SECURITY CONSIDERATIONS AND ENCRYPTION TECHNIQUES

The secrecy and honesty of communications are crucial in tactical operations carried out by law enforcement and military personnel. The interception or compromise of sensitive information can have serious consequences, jeopardizing operational security and putting lives at risk. Security measures and encryption techniques must be implemented to secure Baofeng radio transmissions.

Unencrypted radio transmissions are susceptible to interception by anyone with a compatible receiver tuned to the same frequency. This vulnerability poses severe risks, especially in scenarios where sensitive information, tactical strategies, or personal safety is involved. Encryption encodes the transmitted data, making it unintelligible to unauthorized recipients, mitigating the risks of information leaks, and ensuring communication confidentiality.

Security Challenges

The responsibilities of law enforcement and military personnel involve handling sensitive information and critical operations, making secure communications an absolute necessity. These professionals face unique security challenges in maintaining the confidentiality and integrity of their radio transmissions, as any breach could have severe consequences.

Let's go through the most important threat they may encounter:

- **Interception and eavesdropping**

Radio transmissions can be intercepted by hostile entities. Unencrypted transmissions can be monitored by anyone with a compatible receiver, allowing adversaries to gain valuable intelligence, compromise operational security, or endanger personnel safety.

In law enforcement scenarios, such as undercover operations or high-risk apprehensions, compromised communications could jeopardize the mission, put officers in harm's way, or enable criminals to evade capture. Similarly, in military contexts, intercepted transmissions could reveal strategic plans, troop movements, or other sensitive information to enemy forces.

- **Radio jamming and denial of service**

Adversaries may also attempt to disrupt radio communications through jamming techniques or denial-of-service attacks. By transmitting noise or interference on the same frequencies used for critical communications, they can degrade or completely block the conveying of messages.

Such disruptions can have severe consequences, hindering coordination efforts, cutting off vital lines of communication, and potentially jeopardizing the success of operations or the safety of personnel in the field.

- **Authentication and non-repudiation**

Maintaining the integrity of radio communications is equally crucial. Law enforcement and military personnel must make sure that the messages they receive are authentic and have not been tampered with or spoofed by malicious actors.

Furthermore, certain situations may require non-repudiation. This signature or identification proves who created the message. This feature is particularly important in scenarios involving legal proceedings, evidence gathering, or situations where accountability is essential.

- **Regulatory Compliance and Operational Security**

Beyond the technical challenges, law enforcement and military personnel must also navigate complex regulatory frameworks and operational security protocols. Secure communications must comply with relevant laws, regulations, and organizational policies, which may vary depending on the jurisdiction or operational context.

Failing to follow these regulations could result in legal consequences or compromise operational security, potentially putting personnel and missions at risk. Proper training, documented procedures, and stringent adherence to security protocols are essential for maintaining secure communications in high-stakes situations.

Implementing Encryption

The following steps may be required to implement encryption features and secure Baofeng radio transmissions.

1. Consult with security experts or communication specialists to determine the appropriate encryption techniques and protocols for your specific operational requirements and threat landscape.

2. Ensure compatibility with your Baofeng radio models by obtaining and configuring any necessary encryption modules or hardware.

3. Program encryption keys, algorithms, and security settings into the radios or encryption modules, following proper key management practices to maintain confidentiality.

4. To ensure that encryption is functioning correctly and authorized personnel can communicate securely without issues, conduct thorough testing and verification.

5. Maintain operational security by implementing strict security procedures for handling encryption keys, changing or updating them as necessary

Maintain communication security by providing comprehensive training to personnel on the proper use and configuration of encryption features.

Encryption Techniques

By understanding these security challenges and implementing robust encryption techniques, Baofeng radios can provide law enforcement and military personnel with the necessary tools to safeguard their communications, ensuring confidentiality, integrity, and operational security in even the most demanding situations.

Built-in encryption features

Many Baofeng radio models come equipped with these functionalities integrated into their firmware. These features generally employ industry-standard encryption algorithms, such as Advanced Encryption Standard (AES) or Data Encryption Standard (DES), to encode transmissions.

To activate built-in encryption on your Baofeng radio, follow these steps:

1. Access the encryption menu by pressing [MENU] and navigating to the "Encryption" option.

2. Select the desired encryption algorithm (e.g. AES-128, AES-256, DES).

3. Set a unique encryption key, which must be shared with all radios supposed to participate in secure communication.

4. Enable encryption mode by toggling the appropriate setting.

Once enabled, all transmissions from your radio will be encrypted using the selected algorithm and encryption key, ensuring that only authorized recipients with the correct key can decipher the communications.

External encryption modules

For enhanced security or specific operational requirements, Baofeng offers external encryption modules that can be integrated with your radio. These modules typically provide more advanced encryption algorithms, higher key lengths, and additional security features like key management and over-the-air rekeying.

External encryption modules connect to your Baofeng radio through appropriate interfaces (e.g., USB, serial port) and work in conjunction with the radio's firmware to encrypt and decrypt transmissions seamlessly.

Here is a step-by-step process to set it up:

1. Procure the appropriate encryption module compatible with your Baofeng radio model.

2. Follow the manufacturer's instructions to physically connect the module to your radio.

3. Configure the encryption settings within the module's software or interface, including selecting the desired encryption algorithm, setting encryption keys, and enabling encryption mode.

4. Ensure that all radios participating in secure communication are equipped with compatible encryption modules and configured with the same encryption settings.

Advances encryption algorithms

While the built-in encryption features and basic external modules provide a good level of protection, certain high-risk operations may require more advanced encryption algorithms and longer key lengths to strengthen security.

- **AES-256**

The Advanced Encryption Standard (AES) with a 256-bit key length is one of the most powerful encryption algorithms available. Approved by the U.S. National Security Agency for protecting classified data, AES-256 provides an extremely high level of cryptographic protection.

Baofeng offers specialized external encryption modules that implement AES-256, making this military-grade encryption accessible for professional and commercial applications that require top-tier safeguards.

- **2. Suite B Cryptography**

Suite B is a set of cryptographic algorithms approved by the National Security Agency (NSA) for protecting national security systems and information. It includes advanced algorithms like Elliptic Curve Diffie-Hellman (ECDH) for key exchange, Elliptic Curve Digital Signature Algorithm (ECDSA) for digital signatures, and AES for encryption.

Integrating Suite B cryptography into your Baofeng radio communications through compatible external modules can provide strong end-to-end encryption, authentication, and non-repudiation features.

Frequency hopping and spread spectrum techniques

An additional layer of security can be provided by constantly changing the transmission frequency or spreading the signal across a wider bandwidth. These methods make it harder for adversaries to pick up or block the signal.

Key Management

Effective key management is crucial for maintaining the integrity of any encryption system. Encryption keys must be securely generated, distributed, and updated regularly to prevent potential compromises.

Baofeng's advanced encryption modules often include key management features, such as:

- **Over-the-Air Rekeying (OTAR)**: Allows encryption keys to be updated wirelessly, without the need for physical access to each radio.
- **Key Fill Devices**: Dedicated devices for securely loading encryption keys into ra-

dios or encryption modules.

- **Key Management Facilities**: Software applications or dedicated systems for centralized key generation, distribution, and lifecycle management.

Secure Voice and Data Transmission

While encryption protects the confidentiality of your radio transmissions, additional security measures may be necessary to ensure integrity and authentication.

Secure Voice Transmission

Baofeng's advanced encryption modules often include secure voice features, such as:

- **Digital Voice Encryption**: Applies encryption algorithms specifically designed for voice data, ensuring clear and secure voice communications.
- **Voice Authentication**: Confirms the identity of the speaker through biometric or cryptographic techniques, preventing unauthorized access.

Secure Data Transmission

Many operations also require secure transmission of data. Baofeng's encryption solutions can secure various types of information, including:

- **Encrypted Messaging**: Allows secure exchange of text messages or short data bursts between radios.
- **File Encryption**: Enables secure file transfers, ensuring the confidentiality of sensitive documents.
- **Telemetry Data Encryption**: Protects the integrity of telemetry data, critical for monitoring systems or remote asset tracking.

COMSEC

COMSEC, or Communications Security, is a field within information security that focuses on protecting the confidentiality, integrity, and availability of communications. It involves measures and controls taken to deny unauthorized individuals access to telecommunications and ensure the authenticity of such communications. This includes a range of processes, techniques, and technologies, designed to safeguard communication channels from interception, tampering, and disruption.

COMSEC is crucial for military, government, and commercial entities to ensure that sensitive information communicated over various channels remains secure and confidential.

Its components include:

- **Cryptography**: The use of algorithms and protocols to encrypt communications, making them unreadable to unauthorized parties.
- **Transmission Security (TRANSEC)**: The measures are meant to protect transmissions from interception and exploitation by ensuring secure communication channels.
- **Emission Security (EMSEC)**: These techniques are set to prevent unauthorized interception and analysis of emissions from electronic equipment.
- **Physical Security**: These strategies are made up to protect communication equipment and infrastructure from physical threats, theft, and damage.
- **Key Management**: It refers to all the processes and protocols generating, distributing, storing, and managing cryptographic keys.

Law enforcement and military personnel can significantly enhance the security of their Baofeng radio communications by implementing powerful encryption techniques and sticking to rigorous security protocols. This will mitigate the risks of interception, unauthorized access, and other threats that could compromise sensitive transmissions or jeopardize operational success.

Remember, encryption is only effective when used in conjunction with proper key management practices and adhering to relevant security protocols. Baofeng recommends consulting with security experts or relevant authorities to make sure you comply with applicable regulations and best practices for secure radio communications.

TRAINING AND OPERATIONAL READINESS

Comprehensive training and a high degree of readiness are crucial for the successful integration of Baofeng radios into law enforcement and military operations. Proper instruction ensures that personnel are proficient with these radios and are capable of employing tactical communication tactics, while ongoing preparedness measures safeguard against malfunctions or mishaps during operations.

In this section, we will go through training practices tailored to law enforcement and military communication needs, scenario-based exercises for skills mastery, and operational readiness strategies to enhance the features of Baofeng radio systems.

The Importance of Training

Communication is key in high-stakes situations, and even the latest tech can fail if people do not get it right. Effectively operating Baofeng radios requires far more than a basic understanding of the equipment. Law enforcement and military personnel must receive specialized training that includes the knowledge and skills necessary for clear and secure communications in high-stress operational environments.

1. **Radio operation and configuration**: Personnel must receive thorough instruction on the operation, programming, and configuration of Baofeng radios. This curriculum should include setting frequencies, encryption settings, and integrating with other communication systems.

2. **Tactical communication procedures**: Training should emphasize proper communication protocols, such as using call signs, implementing radio discipline, and following the established communication hierarchies and protocols. Trainees must learn to convey messages with brevity using specific terminology and following COMSEC practices.

3. **Security and encryption protocols**: Encryption techniques and security protocols must be taught in depth to the personnel to safeguard information confidentiality and integrity during operations.

4. **Scenario-based exercises**: While classroom instruction lays the theoretical foundation, scenario-based training exercises are crucial for developing practical skills and preparing personnel for real-world challenges. These exercises can include simulated missions, emergency situations, and challenging communication scenarios, allowing personnel to practice their skills in a controlled setting.

Scenario-Based Training Exercises

Training exercises based on scenarios are especially useful for authorities and military personnel, as they allow for the creation of realistic operational environments and obstacles. They can be designed to replicate various scenarios, such as:

1. **Tactical operations**: Simulating missions like hostage rescue, reconnaissance, or counterterrorism operations, where effective communication is critical for coordination and situational awareness.

2. **Communication failures**: Introducing scenarios where communication systems fail or are disrupted, requiring personnel to improvise and employ contingency plans.

3. **Hostile environments**: Simulating situations with signal interference, jamming, or interception attempts, testing personnel's ability to maintain secure and re-

liable communications.

4. **Multi-agency coordination**: Exercises involving multiple agencies or units, requiring personnel to integrate and communicate across different communication systems and protocols.

Performing these scenario-based exercises on a regular basis allows personnel to sharpen their abilities, uncover potential weaknesses or areas for improvement, and ensure a high degree of operational preparedness.

Maintaining Operational Readiness

In addition to comprehensive training, law enforcement, and military units must implement measures to maintain operational readiness for their Baofeng radios and communication systems. These measures may include:

1. **Regular equipment inspections**: Conduct routine inspections and maintenance on Baofeng radios, ensuring they are in proper working condition and equipped with the necessary accessories, such as antennas, batteries, and encryption modules.

2. **Firmware updates**: Monitoring and implementing firmware updates from Baofeng to address security vulnerabilities, bug fixes, performance enhancements, and new feature releases.

3. **Preventive Maintenance**: Follow the recommendations of Baofeng in terms of maintenance schedules for radios, batteries, and accessories. As we already stated before, proper care extends your device's lifespan and reduces unexpected downtime.

4. **Troubleshooting and reparation**: Develop structured processes for rapidly identifying, troubleshooting, and resolving equipment shortcomings. Always keep on hand some spare radios for immediate swaps when needed.

5. **Proficiency assessments**: Periodically evaluating personnel's proficiency in radio operation, communication procedures, and adherence to protocols through written or practical assessments.

6. **Contingency planning**: Developing and regularly reviewing contingency plans for communication failures or equipment malfunctions, ensuring personnel is prepared to adapt and maintain operational continuity.

7. **Documentation and Accountability**: Maintain up-to-date documentation including equipment inventories, operating procedures, maintenance logs, handling protocols for controlled items (encryption keys, COMSEC), and post-event reports. All this information will help you continue to enhance your proficiency

when it comes to operating your radio device.

8. **Progress Monitoring and Improvement Cycles**: Continuously monitor operational readiness status through data analysis, assessments, and rigorous after-action reviews. Develop corrective action plans to update training, upgrade equipment, enhance processes, and drive continuous improvement.

Law enforcement and military units can maximize the effectiveness of their Baofeng radio communication systems by prioritizing training and operational readiness. This will ensure personnel are well-equipped to handle the demands of tactical operations.

Collaboration with Other Agencies

Law enforcement and military operations often require interagency coordination and unified response abilities. Joint training initiatives can build interoperability. It will simulate a multi-disciplinary, unified response to major incidents like active shooters or disaster scenarios. They also collaboratively develop standardized communication protocols, codes, brevity terminology, and common processes enabling coordinated operations.

The tactical applications of Baofeng radios in law enforcement and military operations emphasize the critical importance of effective and secure communication in high-stakes environments. Their versatility, affordability, and robust capabilities, have proven to be invaluable assets in facilitating coordination, situational awareness, and operational success.

The various aspects of integrating Baofeng radios into tactical communication systems have been explored throughout this chapter. These radios enable seamless coordination during reconnaissance missions, special operations assaults, and other critical operations, according to real-world case studies.

The crucial integration of Baofeng radios with existing communication infrastructures and systems has been emphasized, highlighting the necessity for interoperability solutions and the capability to interface with digital networks, satellite communication systems, and encrypted channels. This fusion not only enhances connectivity and adaptability but also safeguards delicate data from being uncovered or compromised.

Furthermore, the chapter has stressed the importance of comprehensive training and maintaining operational readiness. Law enforcement and military personnel can improve their skills through scenario-based exercises, regular equipment checks, and proficiency assessments.

The capabilities of Baofeng radios can provide a significant advantage as agencies and units navigate the complexities of modern tactical operations. These radios offer a powerful and cost-effective solution for enhancing communication effectiveness, operational security, and overall mission success. They offer a powerful and cost-effective solution for enhancing communication effectiveness, operational security, and overall mission success.

Law enforcement and military agencies must harness the potential of Baofeng radios, integrating them into their communication networks and providing staff with the necessary education and assistance. This will allow them to harness the power of dependable, safe, and versatile communication, allowing their personnel to execute operations with greater coordination, awareness of their surroundings, and ultimately, a greater chance of achieving their objectives.

CHAPTER 6: TROUBLESHOOTING AND MAINTENANCE

Baofeng radios are designed to withstand extreme operational environments. However, as with any sophisticated electronic device, they may encounter issues or experience performance degradation over time. Taking a proactive approach to fixing issues and taking care of your Baofeng radio is crucial for keeping it running for a long time.

We will explore the essential aspects of identifying, diagnosing, and resolving common issues that may arise during the use of Baofeng radios. Additionally, we will provide comprehensive guidance on preventative maintenance practices, ensuring that your radio remains in peak condition and ready for action when you need it the most.

Troubleshooting is an important facet of owning a radio device, as it empowers you to address problems promptly and minimize downtime. Understanding the underlying causes of issues and adhering to organized troubleshooting protocols can often resolve issues without the need for expert assistance, preserving precious time and money.

Implementing a regular maintenance routine is equally important. Proper care not only helps extend the lifespan of your Baofeng radio but also helps maintain its performance and reliability. If maintenance is neglected, it can lead to premature component failure, compromised signal quality, and potentially costly repairs or replacements.

We will now provide you with the knowledge and skills necessary to troubleshoot and keep up your Baofeng radio. They are the key to taking a proactive approach, ensuring that your radio remains a reliable companion, ready to serve you in any situation.

IDENTIFYING AND FIXING COMMON ISSUES

Even the most reliable Baofeng radios may encounter issues during their operational lifespan. Being able to identify and troubleshoot these common problems is crucial for preserving peak performance and saving time. In this section, we will guide you through the process of diagnosing and resolving some of the most frequently encountered issues with Baofeng radios.

Identifying Common Issues

Identifying the problem you are encountering is crucial before attempting to resolve it. Common issues you may encounter include:

1. Poor reception or weak signal strength

2. Audio distortion or interference

3. Keypad or button malfunctions

4. Display issues or error messages

5. Battery life or charging problems

6. Programming or configuration errors

Accurately identifying the issue speeds up the troubleshooting procedure and boosts the odds of a successful resolution.

Troubleshooting Techniques

Once you have identified the problem, it is time to employ effective troubleshooting techniques to diagnose the root cause. Here are some commonly used techniques:

1. **Check the antenna connections**: Make sure it is securely connected and not damaged.

2. **Adjust squelch settings**: Poor reception or unwanted noise can be caused by incorrect squelch settings.

3. **Reset to factory defaults**: Resetting the radio to its original settings can fix software glitches or configuration issues.

4. **Check battery health**: Charge the battery or replace it if it is not holding a charge properly.

5. **Inspect for physical damage**: Look for signs of wear, cracks, or other physical damage that may be causing issues.

6. **Update firmware**: Outdated firmware can sometimes cause compatibility or performance problems.

Step-by-Step Troubleshooting Procedures

To simplify the troubleshooting process, we are now going to provide you with step-by-step procedures and decision trees for some common issues.

1. Poor Reception or Weak Signal Strength

Check the antenna's connection and make sure it's securely fastened. Adjust the squelch level or move to a different location with better signal coverage if the issue persists. The radio should be reset to factory defaults and the firmware should be updated if necessary.

2. Audio Distortion or Interference

Check for obstructions or impurities covering the speaker or microphone. Try adjusting the volume or enabling noise-canceling features if the issue persists. Some frequencies or channels may be experiencing issues due to external interference or configuration issues.

3. Keypad or Button Malfunctions

To reset the radio, start by removing the battery and disconnecting any external power sources. Use compressed air or a gentle cloth to scrub the keypad and buttons. The issue may also require the repair or replacement of the keypad on button.

4. Display Issues or Error Messages

Update the firmware or reset the radio to factory defaults. If the issue persists, it can mean that the display or other internal parts are malfunctioning and require an expert fix or replacement.

ROUTINE MAINTENANCE AND BEST PRACTICES

Preventative upkeep is crucial for preserving and sustaining your Baofeng radio. You can keep your radio in tip-top shape by incorporating regular maintenance tasks into your daily routine. In this section, we are going to show you how to take care of your radio.

Routine Maintenance Tasks

Performing the following routine can help avoid common problems and extend the life of your device.

1. **Cleaning the radio:**

   ❖ Use a soft, dry cloth to wipe down the radio's exterior, removing any dirt, dust, or impurities.

   ❖ Use a small brush or compressed air to clean hard-to-reach areas, such as the speaker grille and connection ports.

   ❖ Avoid using harsh chemicals or solvents, as they may damage the radio's casing or internal components.

2. **Inspecting the antenna:**

   ❖ Check the antenna for any signs of damage, such as cracks, bends, or fraying.

   ❖ Make sure the antenna is securely connected to the radio and free of debris or corrosion.

   ❖ If the antenna shows signs of wear or damage, replace it.

3. **Checking battery contacts:**

   ❖ Clean the battery contacts on both the radio and the battery using a clean, dry cloth or a soft-bristled brush.

   ❖ Remove any dirt, impurities, or corrosion that may interfere with proper electrical contact.

4. **Updating firmware:**

   ❖ Regularly check for firmware updates from the manufacturer periodically and install them to ensure optimal performance and security.

   ❖ To avoid potential issues, follow the manufacturers' instructions carefully when updating firmware.

Best Practices for Storage and Transportation

To protect your Baofeng radio from physical damage and environmental exposure, proper storage and transportation practices are essential. Here are some best practices to follow:

1. **Storage:**

   ❖ Store your radio in a cool, dry place, away from direct sunlight or extreme temperatures.

   ❖ To prevent potential leakage or damage, remove the battery from the radio during long periods of storage.

   ❖ Consider using a protective case or pouch to minimize the risk of scratches or impacts.

2. **Transportation:**

   ❖ Use a protective carrying case or pouch when transporting your radio to prevent accidental drops or impacts.

- ❖ Avoid exposing the radio to excessive moisture, dust, or other environmental hazards during transportation.
- ❖ The radio should be securely fastened if carried in a vehicle to avoid becoming a projectile in the event of sudden braking or collisions.

TIPS FOR PROLONGING THE LIFE OF YOUR RADIO

Baofeng radios are built to last, but just like any other electronic device, they can last a lot longer by following the rules of usage and upkeep.

Avoid Overcharging the Battery

One of the most common causes of battery degradation is overcharging. The excess heat generated by a battery can damage the battery cells and reduce their lifespan. When the battery is fully charged, disconnect the radio from the charger, and avoid leaving it connected for a long time.

Protect Against Extreme Temperatures

The internal components of your Baofeng radio can be damaged by exposure to extreme temperatures. High temperatures can cause components to degrade faster, while cold temperatures can drain the battery more quickly and cause condensation issues. Avoid leaving your radio in direct sunlight or exposing it to freezing temperatures for prolonged periods of time.

Prevent Water Damage

Although some Baofeng radios may be water-resistant or waterproof, it is always best to avoid submerging them in water or exposing them to excessive moisture. Water damage can cause rust, short circuits, and permanent damage to internal parts. Before attempting to use your radio again, remove the battery and allow it to dry thoroughly.

Use Proper Handling Techniques

Proper handling and application methods can greatly reduce the risk of damage to your radio hardware. Internal components or the casing can be damaged by dropping or subjecting your radio to excessive impacts. Furthermore, carefully connecting or disconnecting antennas, cables, and accessories prevents damaging the connection ports.

Regularly Clean and Inspect Your Radio

Cleaning and examining frequently can catch small problems at an early stage. Use a soft, dry cloth to wipe down the radio's exterior and remove dirt and impurities. Check the casing, antenna, and connection ports for signs of wear, cracks, or corrosion. Taking care of small issues right away can keep them from turning into bigger, more costly ones.

Store Your Radio Properly

When not in use, store your Baofeng radio in a cool, dry place, away from direct sunlight or extreme temperatures. A protective case or pouch can help minimize the risk of scratches or impacts during storage. The battery should also be removed from the radio during extended periods of storage to prevent leakage or damage.

Remember that proper maintenance and responsible usage practices are key to getting the most out of your investment and avoiding costly repairs or replacements down the line.

ADVANCED TROUBLESHOOTING TECHNIQUES

While basic troubleshooting techniques can resolve many common issues with Baofeng radios, you may also encounter more complex problems that require advanced troubleshooting approaches. Having the right tools and understanding can make a difference in identifying and resolving technical issues.

Diagnostic Tools and Equipment

When basic troubleshooting methods fail to uncover the root cause of a problem, it is time to use specialized diagnostic tools and equipment. These devices can provide valuable insights into the radio's inner workings and aid in pinpointing issues more precisely. Some essential diagnostic tools include:

1. **Multimeter**: For testing and measuring electrical parameters, such as voltage, resistance, and continuity. It can help identify issues with power supplies, battery connections, and internal circuitry.

2. **Signal Analyzer**: This specialized device enables you to analyze and visualize radio frequency (RF) signals. It can help identify issues related to signal strength, modulation, and interference, which can be particularly useful for troubleshooting antenna or transmission problems.

3. **Programming Cables and Software**: Dedicated programming cables and software are invaluable for diagnosing and resolving issues related to radio configuration or firmware. You can update firmware and perform diagnostic tests with these tools.

Using these advanced diagnostic devices requires specialized skills and training, but they can offer priceless insights and aid you in identifying and resolving intricate issues that may be hard to spot using standard troubleshooting techniques.

Advanced Troubleshooting Techniques

Several methods that can be employed to address complex issues with Baofeng radios:

1. **Component-Level Troubleshooting**: In some cases, the root cause of an issue may lie within a specific component or circuit board. Advanced troubleshooting may involve inspecting, testing, and potentially replacing individual components to identify and resolve the problem.

2. **Firmware Analysis and Debugging**: If the issue seems to be related to firmware or software, advanced troubleshooting may involve analyzing and debugging the firmware code, identifying potential bugs or compatibility issues, and applying patches or updates to resolve the problem.

3. **Reverse Engineering**: In rare cases, when documentation or technical support is limited, reverse engineering techniques may be necessary to understand the radio's internal workings and identify potential issues or solutions.

Seeking Professional Assistance

While advanced troubleshooting techniques can be valuable, there may be situations where the issue exceeds your expertise or capabilities. In such cases, seeking professional assistance from qualified technicians or contacting Baofeng's customer support can be the most efficient path to resolving the problem.

1. **Local Radio Repair Services**: These technicians specializing in two-way radio repair and upkeep can be found in numerous locales. These experts possess the knowledge, skills, and practical experience to identify and resolve challenging issues that may be beyond the scope of routine troubleshooting. List of Baofeng's authorized dealers: https://baofengtech.com/authorized-distributors/

2. **Baofeng Customer Support**: Baofeng offers customer support services to assist with troubleshooting and repair. Their technical support team can provide guidance, firmware updates, and resources to help resolve issues with their products.

Baofeng's customer service email address: support@baofengradio.com

When seeking professional assistance, be prepared to provide detailed information about the issue, including any error messages, symptoms, and steps you have already taken to troubleshoot the problem. This information can help the technicians or support staff better understand the issue and provide targeted solutions.

Even the most complex issues with your Baofeng radio can be addressed by mastering advanced troubleshooting techniques, leveraging diagnostic tools, and knowing when to seek professional assistance.

We took time to explore the critical importance of troubleshooting and maintenance

in preserving the functionality and longevity of Baofeng radios. Like any sophisticated electronic device, these radios can encounter issues or experience performance degradation over time.

When necessary, you can ensure that your Baofeng radio remains a dependable companion, ready to serve you in any situation by mastering the art of identifying and fixing common problems.

We have compiled thorough manuals for identifying and resolving numerous issues, ranging from poor reception and audio distortion to malfunctioning keypads and display glitches. You now possess step-by-step instructions and decision trees to guide you through these obstacles, minimizing downtime and maximizing the radio's performance.

Furthermore, we have emphasized the importance of preventative maintenance, exploring essential tasks such as cleaning, inspecting components, and following best practices for storage and transportation. Many common issues can be avoided by taking these proactive steps early on in your radio's life.

The advanced techniques we have introduced for those times when you encounter more complex or persistent issues include the use of diagnostic tools, component-level troubleshooting, firmware analysis, and even reverse engineering approaches. Even though these methods require specialized skills and understanding, they can be incredibly helpful in identifying and resolving even the toughest technical issues. Lastly, we are conscious of the possibility of requiring expert guidance at times.

Expert guidance and resources can be crucial for resolving issues beyond the scope of general troubleshooting, whether it is consulting with local radio repair services or contacting Baofeng's customer support.

Remember that your Baofeng radio is an investment in reliable communication, and proper troubleshooting and maintenance are essential to protecting that investment. You can make sure your radio stays a top-notch and reliable tool by embracing the tips and tricks presented in this section.

CHAPTER 7: OFF-GRID COMMUNICATION STRATEGIES

The modern world is highly connected but we often take communication for granted, relying heavily on traditional infrastructure like cellular networks and the Internet. However, there are cases where these systems may become unavailable or unreliable, such as in remote areas, during natural disasters, or in the event of large-scale emergencies. In these off-grid scenarios, alternative communication strategies become crucial for personal safety, as well as for coordinating efforts and staying connected.

Baofeng radios emerge as versatile and reliable tools for establishing robust communication networks in off-grid environments. These radios offer a range of features enabling you to maintain vital lines of communication even in the most challenging situations.

Whether you are an outdoor enthusiast venturing into remote wilderness, a professional working in emergency response or disaster relief, or simply someone seeking a reliable means of communication in case of unforeseen events, harnessing off-grid communication strategies with Baofeng radios can be a game-changer.

ESTABLISHING COMMUNICATION NETWORKS IN OFF-GRID SCENARIOS

A reliable communication network can become life-saving in off-grid environments where traditional communication infrastructure may be unavailable or compromised. The versatility and functionality of Baofeng radios allow for seamless coordination and information exchange among group members or responders.

Picking the right frequencies and channels is one of the key strategies for establishing communication networks in such circumstances. Depending on your location and operational needs, the VHF and UHF bands may be a good fit for local communication. For example, the GMRS (General Mobile Radio Service) and FRS (Family Radio Service) frequencies can be used for personal and group communication.

When setting up your communication network, it is essential to establish protocols and assign roles to maintain an organized flow of information. Specific channels or frequencies should be designated for different purposes, such as general communication, emergency alerts, or coordination among specialized teams. To ensure effective information transmission and coordination among group members, you may assign roles like network coordinators.

Furthermore, it is important to establish contact schedules and protocols for maintaining communication. Regular check-in times and predetermined communication windows help to make sure that vital information is shared promptly and that all members remain informed and involved. A common understanding of communication protocols, such as the use of call signs, procedure words, and emergency codes, will facilitate effective and efficient communication.

By leveraging the capabilities of Baofeng radios and implementing strategies for establishing communication networks, you can maintain reliable and robust lines of communication, even in the most challenging off-grid scenarios.

Backup Power Solutions and Battery Management

A reliable power source for your Baofeng radios is essential for effective communication in off-grid environments. Without access to traditional power grids, maintaining a consistent supply of energy becomes a critical consideration. Fortunately, several backup power options exist to keep your radio operational in these situations.

Your Baofeng radios can be charged on the go with portable power banks and external battery packs. These compact and lightweight devices can provide multiple charge cycles, ensuring extended runtime for your radios. Moreover, solar chargers offer a sustainable and eco-friendly alternative, harnessing the sun's energy to power up your device which makes them ideal for extended off-grid operations.

In case of more demanding situations or extended off-grid deployments, hand-crank generators can be a valuable investment. These manual generators convert physical effort into electrical energy, allowing you to charge your radios and other devices without relying on external power sources.

Effective battery management practices are important to complement these backup power solutions. Boosting battery life can make your Baofeng radios last longer, ensuring continuous communication during critical off-grid operations.

Consider implementing power-saving strategies, such as reducing display brightness, disabling unnecessary features, and minimizing transmission time when possible. Additionally, explore the low-power or battery-saver modes available on your Baofeng radios, which can significantly reduce power consumption without compromising essential functionality.

It is also recommended to carry spare batteries and implement a battery rotation schedule. By regularly replacing low-power batteries with fully charged ones, you can ensure continuous radio functionality, minimizing downtime, and ensuring seamless interaction within your off-grid network.

Baofeng radios can provide reliable communication in even the most demanding off-grid scenarios by combining backup power solutions and implementing effective battery management practices.

EFFECTIVE USE OF RADIOS DURING DISASTERS AND EMERGENCIES

In critical situations, reliable communication is paramount for coordinating response efforts, disseminating critical information, and ensuring the safety of both first responders and affected communities. Baofeng radios have emerged as invaluable tools in these high-stakes situations, offering a robust and versatile means of communication when traditional infrastructure may be compromised or overwhelmed.

Radio communication devices can be a great help for real-time coordination and situational awareness during natural disasters like hurricanes, quakes, or wildfires. First responders can use these devices to share vital information, request assistance, and coordinate evacuation efforts. This ensures a unified and effective response to the unfolding crisis.

Similarly, in case of public safety incidents, such as terrorist attacks or civil unrest, Baofeng radios can provide a reliable communication lifeline for law enforcement, medical personnel, and other services involved in the response. Long-range capabilities and robust signal strength enable maintaining communication even in areas where cellular networks may be overwhelmed or disabled.

Baofeng radios can also become a vital link between affected communities and emergency services during power outages or widespread infrastructure failures. Essential communication channels can be maintained by local authorities using these radios to issue evacuation orders and coordinate relief efforts.

Real-life examples and case studies have demonstrated the effectiveness of Baofeng radios in emergency communication scenarios. During Hurricane Katrina in 2005, amateur radio operators played a crucial role in relaying vital information and coordinating rescue efforts, filling the communication gap left by the failure of traditional infrastructure. efforts, filling the communication gap left by the failure of traditional infrastructure. Similarly, during the 2011 Tōhoku earthquake and tsunami in Japan, handheld radios were instrumental in facilitating communication among first responders and affected communities, enabling critical information sharing and coordination of relief efforts.

Establishing clear communication protocols, identifying dedicated channels or frequencies for emergency use, and ensuring that all relevant personnel are trained to properly use and operate these radios are all necessary to maximize the effectiveness of Baofeng radios during disasters and catastrophes. Community and emergency responders can enhance their resilience and preparedness by exploiting the capabilities of Baofeng radios and implementing robust emergency communication strategies.

INTEGRATION WITH EMERGENCY PREPAREDNESS PLANS

Effective emergency preparedness is crucial for minimizing the impact of disasters and ensuring the safety of individuals, families, and organizations. Baofeng radios can serve as a reliable communication solution in the event of disruptions to traditional infrastructure.

It is crucial to include these devices when setting emergency plans and communication strategies. Other crucial items like food, water, first aid supplies, and power sources should also be taken into account. Integrating Baofeng radios into your emergency kit ensures having a means of communication even in the most challenging off-grid situations.

Furthermore, it is recommended that you designate specific Baofeng radio models and frequencies for emergency use within your preparedness plan. This will ensure that all members of your group or organization are operating on the same wavelength.

Regular drills and training exercises are also crucial for ensuring the team's readiness and the effective integration of Baofeng radios into your strategy. Set up and operate your devices, practice emergency communication protocols, and simulate off-grid communication scenarios. These exercises will help identify potential areas for improvement and reinforce the proper use of radio devices in emergency situations.

Individuals, families, organizations, and businesses can enhance their resilience and ability to respond effectively in the face of disasters by integrating Baofeng radios into comprehensive emergency preparedness plans as well as this training routine. This will facilitate the dissemination of critical information, the coordination of response efforts, and ultimately the protection of lives and property.

In case of emergencies or when traditional infrastructure is compromised, off-grid communication strategies are essential. The versatility, dependability, and toughness of Baofeng radios have proven to be invaluable in these situations.

Incorporating off-grid communication tactics is a game-changer for anyone interested in exploring remote wilderness, a professional involved in emergency response or disaster relief efforts, or an individual looking to improve their preparedness. Baofeng radios provide a reliable means of communication, enabling coordination, and information sharing, and ultimately, ensuring the security and well-being of individuals and communities.

Throughout this last chapter, we have explored various strategies for establishing effective communication networks, leveraging backup power solutions, and optimizing battery management practices. The critical role of Baofeng radios in disaster response efforts and their integration into comprehensive emergency preparedness plans have been discussed.

Embrace the knowledge and strategies presented in this chapter and incorporate them into your emergency preparedness plans and off-grid communication protocols. Regular drills and training exercises will help you harness the operation of Baofeng radios and refine your off-grid communication strategies.

Remember that preparedness is key to overcoming communication challenges and ensuring your group's safety in the face of adversity. Thanks to Baofeng radios, you will be able to navigate even the most challenging situations with confidence. These devices will help you keep vital communication lines open and facilitate efficient coordination and response efforts.

Invest in these versatile radios, master their capabilities, and incorporate them into your emergency plans. These extremely powerful devices can really make a difference when conventional communication infrastructure fails. Embrace the adventure of off-grid communication, and rest assured that, with Baofeng radios, you will stay connected and informed, no matter the challenges that lie ahead.

CONCLUSION: STAYING CONNECTED WHEN IT COUNTS

As we reach the conclusion of this comprehensive guide, it is important to reflect on the invaluable knowledge and skills you have acquired throughout your journey with Baofeng radios. Thanks to all the resources provided in this manual, you are now equipped with all the tools you need to unlock the full potential of your two-way radio and stay connected in any situation.

From the very beginning, we have emphasized the importance of understanding the fundamentals of radio communication. You have gained an understanding of the complexities of radio waves, frequencies, and the various components that make up a two-way radio system. This basic knowledge has enabled you to make informed decisions, optimize your radio's performance, and troubleshoot issues effectively.

As you progressed through the chapters, you gained a practical understanding of the advanced functions and features of your Baofeng radio. You can now navigate easily through the radio's menu, program channels, and privacy codes, and harness advanced capabilities such as scanning, tone squelching, and voice encryption. These skills have transformed your radio from a simple communication device into a powerful tool capable of meeting your specific needs and preferences.

We have explored the numerous applications of Baofeng radios, catering to the diverse requirements of outdoor enthusiasts, law enforcement professionals, and military personnel. Your radio device has become an indispensable ally, whether you are an avid hiker looking to stay connected in remote wilderness areas, a law enforcement officer coordinating tactical operations, or a member of the armed forces conducting critical missions.

For outdoor enthusiasts, we have provided guidance on how to leverage your radio for finding your way, coordinating a group, and communicating in case of emergency. You now understand the importance of proper radio etiquette, channel selection, and transmission techniques to ensure seamless communication and safety in the great outdoors.

Regarding the concerns of military law enforcement agencies, we have delved into the tactical applications of Baofeng radios. You have gained insights into secure communication protocols, covert operations, and situational awareness tactics. Your device has become a powerful tool for coordinating teams, handling crises, and safeguarding personnel in high-risk environments.

Furthermore, we have introduced you to the concept of off-grid communication strategies, empowering you to maintain reliable connections even in the absence of traditional communication infrastructure. Whether faced with natural disasters, power outages, or other emergencies, your radio can serve as a lifeline, keeping you informed and connected when it matters most.

However, the knowledge you acquire from this guide is only the beginning of your journey. You need to keep working on your Baofeng radio and getting ready for whatever comes up. Review the techniques and procedures in this manual to put your skills to the test in controlled environments.

Effective communication can make a difference in critical situations. Keeping up with your Baofeng radio skills keeps you ahead of the game no matter what happens. Regularly participate in drills, simulations, or practical exercises, whether with fellow outdoor enthusiasts, law enforcement colleagues, or emergency response teams, to reinforce your skills and identify areas for improvement.

We encourage you to take advantage of more resources and learning opportunities to enhance your abilities. Join local groups or online communities devoted to two-way radio communication, where you can share your tales, learn from others, and keep up with the latest happenings. You can learn a lot from these communities, and improve your radio skills.

Also consider attending workshops, seminars, or specialized training programs offered by experienced instructors or organizations. These educational opportunities can provide practical scenarios, and expert guidance, ensuring that you are well-prepared to handle even the most challenging communication situations.

We also recommend regularly checking the Baofeng website (www.baofengradio.com) and their social media channels for updates, firmware releases, and new product offerings that may further enhance your capabilities. Thanks to Baofeng's commitment to continuous improvement and innovation, you can expect new features, improved performance, and enhanced functionality to be introduced over time.

As technology continues to evolve, staying informed about the latest advancements in radio communication will ensure that you remain at the forefront, equipped with the most up-to-date tools and techniques to stay connected.

Finally, we value your feedback and encourage you to share your experiences with us. Your honest reviews and comments play a crucial role in helping us improve our products and services, ensuring that we continue to provide exceptional value to our customers. Scan the QR code on the back cover of this manual or visit our website's feedback section to leave a comment or offer feedback.

Your thoughts, whether good or bad, will help us pinpoint areas for improvement, address any worries, and ultimately deliver radios and communication tools that better suit your requirements. Incorporating our customers' viewpoints into our product development and support efforts is what we're all about.

Your insights, whether positive or constructive, help us pinpoint areas for improvement, address any concerns, and ultimately deliver radios and communication solutions that better suit your requirements. Incorporating our customers' viewpoints into our product development and support efforts is what matters to us.

Remember that effective communication is a lifeline in critical situations. By embracing the knowledge and skills acquired through this guide, practicing regularly, and staying committed to continuous learning, you will always stay connected whatever the circumstances. Your Baofeng radio is a powerful tool. With perseverance and dedication, you will be able to unlock its full potential, making sure you are always prepared to communicate effectively, no matter what obstacle comes your way.

Embrace the power of two-way radio communication, and let your radio device be your trusted companion on every adventure, mission, or emergency situation. Your ability to communicate effectively will make all the difference when it matters most. Stay connected, stay informed, and stay prepared.

REFERENCES

"Baofeng." n.d. Moonraker (US) Limited. Accessed May 19, 2024. https://moonrakeronline.com/brands/baofeng.

"BaoFeng (UV-5R) 8-Watt Dual Band Two-Way Radio." n.d. I.W.A International Inc. Accessed May 19, 2024. https://iwainternationalinc.com/baofeng-uv-5r-8-watt-dual-band-two-way-radio/.

"Baofeng Radio." n.d. Two Way Radio. Accessed May 19, 2024. https://www.hamtwowayradio.com/product-category/two-way-radio/baofeng-radio/.

"Baofeng Radio Main Page." n.d. Baofeng Radio. https://www.googleadservices.com/pagead/aclk?sa=L&ai=DChcSEwir5NOn0ZmGAxX8RkECHdvDAwkYABAUGgJ3cw&ase=2&gclid=Cj0KC-QjwxqayBhDFARIsAANWRnQBow_fkgKqQC5ITQRj76UYmn04BsLDFLjn3pOaspsI7xaCILERnhYaAj4jE-ALw_wcB&ohost=www.google.com&cid=CAESVuD27SESMpjyEjNQDgRXx7oSTeOovw_6PPLWw_nuH1JUY6KZqQbpWRDu4EfjxS67jFZ0TUfm8_XpGA7brjmLp6iFcHLMOEqblVSfRADHGN1cWP-FZrgl&sig=AOD64_1N8R7JdfaUJ75cUM3VIbT2KrnrFQ&q&nis=4&adurl&ved=2ahUKEwiuzMyn0ZmGA-xXFcfEDHWxFCloQ0Qx6BAgMEAM.

"Baofeng Radio without a Licence | Essex Ham." n.d. Www.essexham.co.uk. Accessed May 19, 2024. https://www.essexham.co.uk/baofeng-radio-without-licence.

2024. Wikipedia. May 14, 2024. https://en.wikipedia.org/wiki/Baofeng_UV-5R.

"BaoFeng UV-5R - Emergency Communication & Frequencies." n.d. Bug out Bag Builder. https://www.bugoutbagbuilder.com/learning-tutorials/baofeng-uv-5r-basic-setup-emergency-frequencies.

"Baofeng UV-5R - the RadioReference Wiki." n.d. Wiki.radioreference.com. Accessed May 19, 2024. https://wiki.radioreference.com/index.php/Baofeng_UV-5R.

"Baofeng UV-5R Can Receive Messages but When I Transmit Back No One Can Hear Anything?" 2023. Two Way Radio Forum. June 21, 2023. https://www.twowayradioforum.com/t/baofeng-uv-5r-can-receive-messages-but-when-i-transmit-back-no-one-can-hear-anything/10490.

"Baofeng/Pofung UV-5R." n.d. Www.eham.net. Accessed May 19, 2024. https://www.eham.net/reviews/detail/10349.

Centers, Josh. 2020. "BaoFengs Are Fine Radios, but They Don't Have Hundreds of Miles of Range." The Prepared. December 4, 2020. https://theprepared.com/blog/baofengs-are-fine-radios-but-they-dont-have-hundreds-of-miles-of-range/.

"Home BaoFeng Radio." n.d. www.baofengradio.co. Accessed May 19, 2024. https://www.baofengradio.co/.

Martens, Michael. 2019. "Should a Baofeng Be Your First Ham Radio?" KB9VBR Antennas. August 28, 2019. https://www.jpole-antenna.com/2019/08/28/should-a-baofeng-be-your-first-ham-radio/.

Pekelny, Jonnie. 2021. "Review: Yaesu FT-60R vs BaoFeng BF-F8HP for New Ham Radio Operators." The Prepared. July 14, 2021. https://theprepared.com/blog/review-yaesu-ft-60r-vs-baofeng-bf-f8hp-for-new-ham-radio-operators/.

SaveNetRadio. 2023. "Best Baofeng Radio in 2023 - Reviews & Buying Guide." SAVENETRADIO. January 19, 2023. https://www.savenetradio.org/best-baofeng-radio/.

Mikael Blomkvist. 28 July 2021, images.pexels.com/photos/8961028/pexels-photo-8961028.jpeg?auto=compress&cs=tinysrgb&w=1260&h=750&dpr=2 . Accessed 11 June 2024.

Cottonbro studio. 22 June 2020, images.pexels.com/photos/4710965/pexels-photo-4710965.jpeg?auto=compress&cs=tinysrgb&w=1260&h=750&dpr=2 . Accessed 11 June 2024.

Quang Nguyen Vinh. 29 Apr. 2020, images.pexels.com/photos/4268181/pexels-photo-4268181.jpeg?auto=compress&cs=tinysrgb&w=1260&h=750&dpr=2 . Accessed 11 June 2024.

Gustavo Fring. 16 Mar. 2021, images.pexels.com/photos/7155794/pexels-photo-7155794.jpeg?auto=compress&cs=tinysrgb&w=1260&h=750&dpr=2 . Accessed 11 June 2024.

macrovector. Météo Icônes Polygonales, img.freepik.com/vecteurs-libre/meteo-icones-polygonales_1284-13362.jpg?t=st=1718099874~exp=1718103474~hmac=8facede15cdbc7163d1bc287f5d079b-9834dc461fd213ad2182ba8145be4ff6f&w=106 0. Accessed 11 June 2024.

Guzman, Art.

images.pexels.com/photos/8079179/pexels-photo-8079179.jpeg?auto=compress&cs=tinysrgb&w=1260&h=750&dpr=2 . Accessed 11 June 2024.

Zern Liew. Concept: Mobile Cell Phone Tower Triangulation. Three Cell Towers with Intersecting Signals.,

as1.ftcdn.net/v2/jpg/03/53/20/50/1000_F_353205079_HeYF0gsTpD73qFL3X8Om0VV5lcDjfCfn.jpg . Accessed 11 June 2024.

Gunzexx Png And Bg. Three Soldiers in Camouflage Gear Are Gathered around a Vehicle, Faces Obscured, in a Military Setting,

as2.ftcdn.net/v2/jpg/08/21/13/77/1000_F_821137783_vxXXPs6ddQLi7vsazer2UnVspu7VUhpl.jpg . Accessed 11 June 2024.

Made in United States
Troutdale, OR
11/19/2024

25035442R10058